MICHAEL,
ALWAYS ON
CORNER! GOST,

FIGHT THE GOOD FIGHT

A Mother's Legacy Lives On

Benjamin A. Newman
Field Director

701 Market St Ste 1070
Saint Louis, MO 63101
314 244 0707 office
314 304 0577 cell
314 244 0796 fax
benjamin.newman@nmfn.com
www.benjamin-newman.com

Fight the Good Fight

A Mother's Legacy Lives On

B.A. Newman
with Mary Beshear

Mill City Press

Copyright © 2009 by B.A. Newman. All rights reserved.

Mill City Press, Inc.
212 3rd Avenue North, Suite 290
Minneapolis, MN 55401
612.455.2294
www.millcitypublishing.com

All rights reserved. No part of this publication may be reproduced, stored in a retrieval system, or transmitted, in any form or by any means, electronic, mechanical, photocopying, recording, or otherwise, without the written prior permission of the author.

ISBN - 978-1-934937-81-5
ISBN - 1-934937-81-9
LCCN - 2009928879

Cover Design by Jenni Wheeler
Typeset by Madge Duffy

Printed in the United States of America

Dedicated to the love of my life
Ami V. Newman

In loving memory of
Janet Fishman Newman

A product of The Continued Fight, LLC
www.continuedfight.com

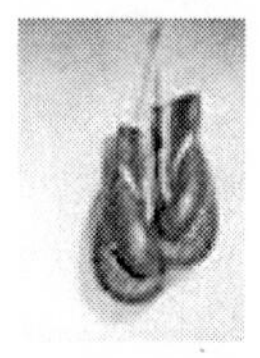

Early praise for *Fight the Good Fight*

"This book really touched me. I believe it will cause you to reflect upon and honor the heroes of your past and inspire you to create your future."

Jon Gordon, Author of *The Energy Bus* and *Training Camp*

"*Fight the Good Fight* will enable you to live with more purpose and conviction and will provide the tools to unleash the champion in you!"

Roland Williams, 8-year NFL veteran & Super Bowl Champion

"*Fight the Good Fight* is a must read. It's a belly punch of inspiration and creativity. You will go 12 rounds with this book and along the way you will be reminded of the importance of family, perseverance, and solid procedural habits in our lives. If you implement only part of what this book offers, you will live a happier and more successful life."

Rudy Telscher, Managing Partner, Harness, Dickey & Pierce
Lead Counsel in CBC v. Major League Baseball

"Ben Newman's passion is contagious, and his conviction is quite powerful. You will go round by round, uncover your purpose for everyday life and learn to embrace the adversity."

Tait Cruse, Managing Partner, Texas Financial Group-Dallas,
Northwestern Mutual Financial Network

"I believe in living *Your Life By Design* and this book will lead you to direction and purpose in fulfilling your legacy."

Curtis Estes, Author of *Your Life by Design*

"We inevitably will face challenges in life. *Fight the Good Fight* will empower you to overcome your obstacles and choose success for your future."

Michael Kennedy, Jr., President, KAI Design & Build

TABLE OF CONTENTS

"I believe I will pull through as long as I keep working at it, where maybe someone else would succumb to it. I just want to grow old with my kids and enjoy their futures."

Janet Fishman Newman

ACKNOWLEDGMENTS

This book is dedicated to my wife, Ami, and is for our son, J. Isaac. The two of you make me better every day and help me understand the importance of love, family and God's work better than any example I have had. This book wouldn't have been possible without both of you. Words can't express how much I love you.

I also want to express my gratitude to the following people:

To my mother, Janet Fishman Newman, you are my inspiration to live each day to the fullest and appreciate life. You taught me that it's not how long you live but how you live your life that matters. Not a day goes by that I don't think of you. I know you are with me always.

Thanks to my mother-in-law, Jean Aden-Olson, for providing enough love to J. Isaac for two grandmothers.

To Carolyn Harris, for your endless love and support when my mother was ill. Your care of and love for me have helped me become the man I am today.

To Jon Gordon, for your courage when you challenge me to grow personally and spiritually. Thank you for your continued support, mentoring and friendship.

To Mary Beshear, for being the loving individual that you are and helping me grow closer to my mother than I ever imagined possible.

To my grandparents, Marcel and Bessie Newman, for your love and examples of hard work; you are forever missed.

To my grandparents, Herman and Shirley Fishman, for your endless love and life lessons. You taught me so much about being a man; every grandchild should be so fortunate. I miss you both so very much.

To Steve and Derry Fishman, for supporting my mother when times were tough and being there for me.

To Barry and Rita Worth for always being there for support and guidance through the years.

To Josh Qualy and Andy Kaiser, my best friends, for your support through the good and the bad. I know I can count on you both for anything.

To Phil and Ilene Kaiser, John and Kathy Qualy, and Carla and Ed Doisy, for your parental support and unconditional love through the years.

Thanks to John O'Leary and Roland Williams, for your friendship and for sharing your powerful life stories for this book.

To Eldad Bialecki and Jonathan Shanker, former students of my mother's who have become personal friends, thank you for sharing your stories of how my mother affected your lives.

To Dr. Martha Skinner, Elaine Ullian and all the doctors, nurses and staff at the Boston Medical Center who helped my mother unleash her positive mental attitude when faced with amyloidosis, I can't thank you enough.

To our many other family and friends, all of whom we love very much, your support and love has helped this book become a reality.

To God, for the purpose You have designed for me. Nothing is possible without Your vision.

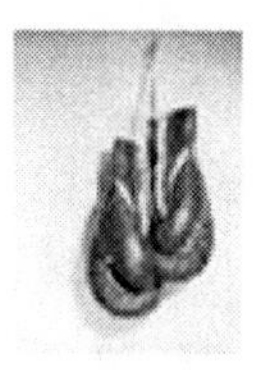

FOREWORD by Jon Gordon

My mother passed away two and half years ago, yet she is with me wherever I go. Her spirit, her love, her influence, her work ethic and her legacy live on through me, through my family, through my books and speaking, and through the life I live. Because of her, I've learned that a mother is not someone who simply brings you into this world, she is someone who prepares you to take on the world. Her strength and courage in the face of cancer will always inspire me, and the love she shared during her life will always influence me. A mother's love makes all the difference.

That's why I love this book. Ben Newman knows he did not become a success by himself. He, like so many of us, is the byproduct of his mother's love, wisdom, guidance, inspiration and legacy — a legacy that lives on through him and comes to life in this wonderful and inspirational story.

Yes, this book is a gift of authenticity, vulnerable inspiration, sincere wisdom and hope in the midst of life's great struggles. Through her journal, which inspired this book, Ben's mom made a gift to him of her life. In turn, he has given all those who read this book the gifts of wisdom and courage required to fight the good fight.

I often say that life can no longer be compared to a marathon or a sprint. Rather, it is more like a series of sprints combined with a boxing match. While we are running the distance, we get hit along the way. All of us will be tested on our journeys, and we must respond to these tests with faith, courage, hope, trust and love. Thank you, Ben, for sharing your story. Thank you for empowering us to face our challenges. Thank you for allowing your mother's legacy to live on through your life and this book. And thank you for encouraging and inspiring us to get up when we've been knocked down so we can continue to fight the good fight.

— Jon Gordon is the author of the International bestseller,
The Energy Bus: Fuel your Life, Work and Team with Positive Energy and Training Camp

PROLOGUE

The first thing people noticed about her was her beauty. She stood out in a crowd. But as any new acquaintance would quickly realize, Janet Newman's physical charm merely decorated a warm, engaging and beautiful spirit.

She was unselfish and servant-hearted in her care for others. She was also wise and disciplined, as well as creative, playful and revered by those who knew her.

She was my mother, and I cherished her with all my heart.

Janet Fishman Newman's death, 11 days before my eighth birthday, left a cavernous hole in my universe.

Several years ago my grandmother gave me a personal gift I treasure — the journal my mom left behind. Within its pages I discovered her legacy of hope, resolve and inspiration. As I share parts of it with you in the ensuing pages, my prayer is that it imparts to you, too, insights and encouragement.

Though the journal was a personal record kept during my mother's medical ordeal and not a memoir written to be read by me or my brother, it is surprisingly full of wisdom that seems meant for us. When I reread her thoughts on how to live as a champion in the midst of struggle, I am as strengthened by her wisdom as if she had written me a personal letter. The following scripture expresses the impact my mom's journal has had on me:

....My son, I give you this instruction ...so that by following [it]...you may fight the good fight, holding onto faith and a good conscience. (I Timothy 1:18)

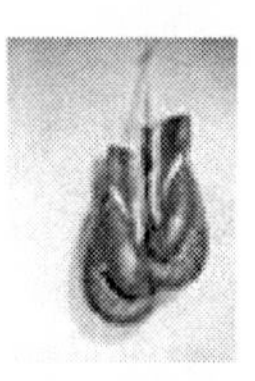

ROUND ONE
Be a Prizefighter

"I was getting upset when talking or thinking about [celebration]s, grandparent[ing], and future things that may not occur. After a couple of weeks at home, I'm concentrating more now on living each day to the fullest and realistically keeping the sad reality in the back of my mind."

Janet Fishman Newman

Life is full of challenges for every person walking this earth. As we daily take these on, the act of living can stretch and even strengthen us. Sometimes our efforts will lead us to achieve measurable and worthy goals. Other times the obstacles are so big, we can't overcome them. Still, we can choose to be a "prizefighter" in the daily challenge to do our best.

My mother, Janet Fishman Newman, was a prizefighter in my eyes. At the age of 33, she experienced the onset of primary amyloidosis, a rare systemic disorder that leads to organ dysfunction. Knowing her life expectancy was a shocking two to four years, my mother fought to have the best quality of life she could with her two boys my brother Andrew and me. She and Dad divorced when I was six months old and Andrew was three, so she was a single parent working to make ends meet. I still marvel at the positive attitude she maintained with all that she managed.

Amyloidosis causes a complex protein (an amyloid) to abnormally build up in one or more tissues and organs, interfering with bodily function and eventually causing the affected organs to shut down. As amyloidosis progresses, the person affected may experience fatigue, weight loss, numbness and tingling in the extremities, shortness of breath, muscle weakness, nausea and eventually chronic and acute pain.

For the four-and-a-half years she struggled with this disease, my mother was in and out of the hospital for tests that are too numerous to count, for procedures that were time-consuming and uncomfortable at best, frightening and painful at their worst. She endured countless blood tests, bone-marrow aspirations, echocardiograms, gallium scans, chest x-rays, skeletal x-rays, liver and spleen scans, gastrointestinal evaluations, angiograms, renal biopsies and heart biopsies.

In the midst of all this, she worked to be as cheerful and energetic as possible for my brother and me. At dinner time, she focused on our day rather than hers, asking questions and showing interest in the details we shared. She placed great importance on the ritual of putting us to bed with favorite stories, special talks and big hugs.

Even though I could not have put it into words at the time, I now realize she was demonstrating an important truth — our circumstances in life are much less significant than our responses to those circumstances. Her actions make me think of Abraham Lincoln's words: "I do the very best I know how — the very best I can; and I mean to keep doing so until the end."[1] When I look back on her calm cheerfulness, I see her as that prizefighter, fighting the good fight to keep our family life balanced and sound.

Many months before the end of her life, my mother was managing a complex regimen of daily medications. She wore a mask in cold weather to protect her lungs and Jobst stockings on her legs to control the tingling and numbness in her lower extremities. She had to sleep so her head was inclined above her chest, and she came to the dinner table every night pulling an IV stand with packs that dripped pain medications into her body. In fact, her bedroom at home was transformed into a hospital room, complete with reclining bed and 24-hour nursing care.

Though she was serene despite these circumstances, I remember the deep sadness that came over me when she could no longer come into our bedroom for story time. Sometimes after I made my way through the tangle of her IV lines to kiss her goodnight, I cried so hard with 8-year-old worry and sorrow that she called my grandparents, Herman and Shirley, asking them to provide the comfort and reassurance she could no longer give.

And even then, I see her as fighting the good fight. She didn't let her inability to comfort me plunge her into a deep depression. She didn't try to play the hero and do something beyond her strength that might have compromised her fragile health. Nor did she complain about my tears or try to shush my emotions; she simply picked up the phone and got me the best help she could … an overnight stay with my wonderful grandparents!

As her illness progressed, my mother had to be more and more intentional in her planning. Eventually, she wisely arranged for us to receive care from a St. Louis social service. The fact that the care came in the form of a woman named Carolyn Harris was an incredible blessing. In many ways, Carolyn was a life saver for our family. I have wonderful memories of Carolyn picking me up from school, of cooking great meals for my mother, Andrew, and me each evening. Working alongside my mother, Carolyn taught me lessons of love and care that have a profound impact on the man I have become today.

I'm told that many people struggling with illness do not take kindly to help when it is extended, finding constant fault with the caregiver and with each detail of care. As I hear such stories, I marvel anew at my mother's grateful heart and at the team spirit she always seemed to display.

Today, when it's culturally acceptable to blame others and to whine about any inconvenient detail, I applaud my mother's positive attitude and team spirit. I don't know if she was an admirer of Teddy Roosevelt, but her clear-eyed practical outlook seems to demonstrate his simple axiom, "Do what you can, with what you have, where you are."[2] I don't believe Roosevelt was talking about heroics; he was talking about simply noticing what's needed and doing what we can with our available resources. Sometimes I wonder how much stronger our communities would be if everyone did what they could.

Examples might be as simple as finding time to call a friend who's going through a hard time, to passing on a favorite book to someone looking for inspiration, lending a hand on a neighborhood project, or perhaps pulling the proverbial weeds in our own yards.

One specific example of Roosevelt's statement and my mother's attitude stands out in my mind. A friend of mine was working her way through college with several jobs, including one which involved washing sheets and linens in a local hotel. Several weeks into the job, she realized she was spending her days in the laundry room feeling sorry for herself. So she stopped the negative thought process and began praying — as she folded linens — for the guests who would use them. The powerful thing about doing what we can with what we have is this: Even small positive actions give *us* an emotional lift, because we sense we are doing something good and meeting a need, too.

My mother remarked in her journal that, during her illness, she had rekindled many friendships for which she had previously not been able to find the time. She wrote, "Why do we <u>not</u> make time for our most important relationships?" I often reflect on my mother's question, because there are stretches in my life when I forget to slow down and enjoy relationships that are precious to me. When I am aware of how sad I am about not being able to converse with my mother face to face (until we meet in Heaven), I strengthen my efforts to cherish important relationships and stay in contact with people who have made an impact on me. This is just one more way we can do what we can, right where we are. In mom's case, she was a big encourager for those around her.

One of the first principles gleaned from my mother as she fought to live is the belief she held that what happens to us is not as important as how we respond to it.

And her healthy responses to the challenges she faced, including allowing others to do what she could not, shows her willingness to "do what she could with what she had." Perhaps these principles seem overly simple. Or they might be the most profound lessons we can learn from on a daily basis.

As you read through the pages of this book, you will

recognize that each chapter, or "round," begins with a quote from my mother's journal. Many of her words are notes to herself, written to impart personal strength and encouragement. Yet, in as much as her notes contain timeless truths, they live on for you and me. Sometimes it takes seeing things written in black and white to realize a hope we have long squelched, to recognize truth, or observe a personal trait we'd like to develop more.

Consequently, each chapter ends with a question to ponder, a question to help you, the reader, uncover strengths and deepen insights. I hope that my words and those of my mother, Janet Fishman Newman, will touch and awaken some chords of blessing in your life or in the lives of your family. Perhaps, for some of you, the timing won't be quite right. And perhaps for others of you, the timing will be perfect and the questions will bring issues you are ready to ponder. Maybe, just maybe … this is your time to open some box of opportunity that's been tucked away on your mental shelf.

Question to ponder:

Are there worthwhile endeavors needing to be done around you that you could easily accomplish with your current resources and within your existing circumstances?

ROUND TWO
A Mother's Journal

"I explained what the disease was to the kids so they could understand that I was very sick and would not get better totally. Andrew asked if I could die. I told him no one knows when anyone will die. He seemed satisfied with that ... for now."

Janet Fishman Newman

I've always believed that everything in life is about timing. As young boys, my brother and I understood as much about our mother's illness as our ages would allow. However, amyloidosis' impact on our family would take years for me to fully understand. And my mother's death, though immediately grievous and shocking when it occurred, is a loss I'm still processing today.

Actually, I believe that everything we take on in life, both personally and professionally, is influenced by an unconscious internal timing. Though we may not be aware of doing so, we instinctively scan issues that come into our realm according to our readiness to take them on. We unconsciously sense whether we have the discipline to deal with a proposed challenge, or the emotional depth to face the intense feelings it may arouse. We might intuitively know there is a huge opportunity before us, but we may not yet have the wisdom to understand it and take it on. Because this assessment happens unconsciously, we may find ourselves shelving an issue for later, though we're not sure why.

That is exactly what happened to me in college. When I was in my junior year at Michigan State University, my grandmother, Shirley, gave me a box of my mother's belongings. Among other personal items in the box was my mom's journal detailing her struggle with amyloidosis, the degenerative disease that took her life. Just having something with her handwriting on it was priceless to me, and I knew the notebook was a treasure. But as a young man, just beginning a college career, I could hardly handle the emotions it aroused. I had read only one page of my mother's descriptions of her physical illness when I began to cry so hard I had to close the journal.

At that point in my life, I somehow knew I hadn't developed the inner strength to receive the blessing that came in a package wrapped so tightly with grief. The timing wasn't right.

So, I put the journal back in the box and for safekeeping, I placed this box in a larger one .... a "Two Men and a Truck" moving box, which I taped closed with a *full* role of duct tape. I'm not sure if I was trying to seal *out* potential moisture damage with the duct tape, or if I was trying to seal *in* this journal that would most assuredly reawaken the pain of my tremendous loss. Whatever my unconscious motives, I moved that box from place to place with me throughout the next years of my life. Looking back, I realize I should have placed the journal in a safety deposit box or certainly in something that would offer more security than a roll of duct tape!

The box, however, remained undisturbed until 2007, when my wife, Ami and I decided to clean out our garage. Ami was pregnant at the time, and we were planning for our son's arrival. Our storage shelves held 25-30 clear plastic tubs and one cardboard box totally wrapped in duct tape. Trying to determine who should tackle which storage bins, Ami looked at me and said, "Honey, what's in that box?" I looked up at the box and began silently to ask myself if I was ready to open it. On this particular Saturday, I sensed the timing was right.

I pulled down the box and cut through the layers of tape. Ignoring all the other contents, I went immediately to my mother's journal. Not knowing the personal treasure hunt I was embarking on, Ami went back into the house to look for something. When she returned, she found me standing in the middle of the garage holding a battered notebook over an equally battered box and crying harder than she'd ever seen me cry.

When she asked what was wrong, all I could do was wordlessly hand the journal to her. Ami sat down on a storage bin in the dusty garage and read the journal from cover to cover, crying all the while, as she began to discern the pain my mother must have felt leaving her sons behind. Carrying a child of her own, Ami found the journal more than difficult to read. When she finished, she said, "You have to be strong enough to read this journal. Your mother has left this for you. It reflects so many of the life principles you believe in and live by. It is full of her ... and you are so much like her."

My wife's words were a salve to a dry and parched part of my psyche. As an adult, I had been longing to know my mom; what she was like, what she stood for, what she valued. And I wanted to know that I was carrying some good part of her legacy into my own family's life. Yet all I had before this day were the foggy memories of an 8-year-old boy whose mother was very sick.

Ami's words propelled me into the journal, reading it page by page. As I read, I was amazed and encouraged to discover all the positive ways my mom's life had affected me in eight short years, so long ago. Growing up without her, I sometimes had felt like a ship at sea without a rudder, a feeling I later came to understand when I heard lectures in college on the value of parental involvement in a child's life. But I know God filled this void by bringing individuals into my life who nurtured me, who helped me meet challenges and who became good examples and role models. I'm humbled and full of gratitude for my grandparents and for so many others who cared for me. I sense that some of my best traits came from examples these adults modeled for me.

After my mother passed away, my father moved back into the family home with Andrew and me. With thoughtful insight, he hired Carolyn Harris to continue to care for us after school each day. Carolyn's presence, along with my dad's, provided caring adult influences.

After reading mom's journal, I was delighted to realize that she, too, had a dynamic impact on me. Her passion for life, her positive attitude, her desire to encourage others, all were traits she had passed on to me without either of us realizing it. I think it was social reformer Henry Ward Beecher who said, "The mother's heart is the child's schoolroom."[1] Thankfully, it seems that can prove true even if a mother's life is cut short. And as is also sometimes true in life, I'm not sure I even recognized her traits in me. Reading her journal brought them to light.

And even though her words were not intended for me, they gave to me an understanding of the characteristics we share.

Questions to ponder:

What circumstances and obstacles have molded your life?

What steps have you taken to get beyond the obstacles?

What quiet characteristics might be lying within you, waiting for an affirmation or verbal description that can bring them to life?

Can you put these traits into words, words that might somehow help you better act on them?

ROUND THREE
Why? Discovering Your Purpose

"Dr. Skinner ... told me that the amyloids are in the plasma of my bone marrow and that I definitely have primary amyloidosis. When I heard this, I was upset because I knew that primary was not as successful as secondary. When he told me my life expectancy was two to four years, I was hysterical. I wouldn't see my kids grow up. They wouldn't have me."

Janet Fishman Newman

The journal reveals what anyone might expect. My mother was hysterical when she learned the news of her life expectancy. But my brother and I never saw her fear and heartache. Instead, she found positive ways every day to manage our household and be active in our lives.

As I come to know my mother through her journal, I'm thankful to have her example of courage. It takes bravery and fortitude to face obstacles like hers head-on and overlook personal fears. I remember a time when my mother and I were riding in the car together. As she drove down the street, I watched her smile and wave at friends. At one point we stopped, and she had a lively conversation with a neighbor. I recall her putting much energy into expressing her interest in our friend, and this was after my mother had become quite sick. She did not focus on her ailments and always seemed to have energy for others.

Her ailments *were* very pressing, however. Our family vacations for a number of years consisted of a trip to Boston, where she could receive treatments for her disease. The Boston Medical Center was one of the few places in the world conducting research on and treating patients with amyloidosis. But even these trips have left me with great memories. There was no talk of pain or complaining about procedures. Instead, my mother found ways to make the trip fun. She insisted, for example, that we eat in Chinatown, because she knew we loved Chinese food. She also took us to Candlestick Bowling, and she strove passionately to bowl strikes each time, just like we boys did.

I remember sitting in a booth at the bowling alley, having a snack between sets, and using paper and pencil to play games of hangman with my mom. She was very intuitive and seemed to know how I thought and how my mind worked. Twice she guessed the word I had chosen while I was still drawing my hang man and filling in my empty lines. My mother and I had a special bond that I will forever cherish.

While my mother received treatments from Dr. Skinner on these trips to Boston, my grandparents, Herman and Shirley, who accompanied us, would make sure Andrew and I had an incredible day planned. Little did I know that these outings would be the beginning of their increasingly important role in my life. I was fortunate that when my mother passed away, my grandparents were there to nurture me and teach me about life.

Though the Boston trips were fun for Andrew and me, I now realize how hard they must have been for my mother. I'm inspired when I think about the energy she spent, when fear and physical limitations were greatly threatening her reserves. Her example puts things into perspective for me when I face obstacles that feel discouraging.

As a life insurance salesman, I face each weekly schedule that needs to be filled with 30 appointments, and I think of my mother's courage. When I face a client with disappointing news that a policy application has been declined, I think of my mom's courage. When I face an afternoon of broken appointments that require follow-up and/or the remarketing of my services, I think of my mother's courage and energy. And my challenges seem more doable. As a father, when I come home from a challenging day at work and realize the most important part of my day is just beginning, I think of my mother's energy.

Most of us go through times when a very real fear fills our gut, and we wonder if we'll be willing to complete the meaningful tasks in front of us. We wonder if we'll be able to dig down deep enough to use our God-given talents and come closer to our capacity. I've heard it said that if people want to keep from being overwhelmed by very real short-term fears and pressures, they need long-range goals. Obviously, my mom had a heavy life-threatening worry weighing on her, but she had even more important long-term goals—keeping our family afloat emotionally, staying healthy as long as she could and making preparations for her children's futures.

These long-term goals were her "why." They were the reasons she got up in the morning. All of us need to recognize our "why." This is true for anyone, from the CEO of a Fortune 500 company down to the entry-level employee working at a first job. All of us need dreams that keep us going, we need the "whys" that motivate us. The best dreams are those that involve a purpose greater than ourselves and stretch us to be the best we can be.

Over the years, I've come to see that one of my personal passions is for helping others. I love to help people discover what's important to them and then support them in making choices that develop and protect their values. I'm fortunate to be able to do this in my career, as well as in my personal life.

However, I realize I have to keep my focus on this "why" to stay motivated, because helping people is not always as easy as it sounds. My job involves making hundreds of phone calls per week, meeting with at least four clients each work day and prepping for those meetings, as well as following up with paperwork. I'm fortunate to have a team to help me with my purpose. Without my staff and their support, I don't think I could impact the large number of people with whom I'm blessed to work each year.

My mother also had a team to keep her focused. Her team was comprised of her physicians, nurses and medical staff. Her journal reveals that she often took time to get to know her team and their motivations, their whys. She recorded notes about people's families, their favorite foods and travel destinations. This is fascinating to me, because she could have been like many patients who never seek positive experiences with those in whom their lives are entrusted. But she was able to see that the technicians were helping her achieve her health goals, and she wanted to encourage them in the things they found important. Medical interactions can be negative and impersonal, but my mother worked to keep them personal and warm.

I think of her when my business interactions get difficult. The truth is: The more interactions a person has each day, the more opportunity he or she has to face rejection or criticism. So it's important for me to stay focused on my goal to help people make choices that develop and protect their values.

As I become more and more clear about my purpose, I've noticed four very real benefits that I believe are true for everyone. Knowing our purpose gives us:

- More courage to take life head-on,
- Greater discipline to stay focused,
- Deeper knowledge of why good habits matter, and
- Clearer vision for the future

Most people's daily work involves at least a few tasks we'd rather not do … but when we see that these chores, rightly done, mount up to a result that matters to us and others, we are motivated to persevere.

Another important factor that keeps the human psyche from being overwhelmed by short-term frustrations is a caring network. We need loved ones whose belief in us serves as encouragement to persevere when the going gets rough. The most significant "whys" in my life are Ami and our son, J. Isaac. Ami is an incredible woman and a great support to me. Every day, when I put on my tie to go to work, she gives me a kiss and every single day, without fail, she looks me square in the eye and says to me, "Honey, GO DO GREAT THINGS!" Her support and inspiration help me live each day in a more purposeful way. And when our son, J. Isaac, who has recently learned to wave bye-bye, smiles and waves to me as I leave for work, it melts my heart and reminds me why I do what I do.

Years ago, American psychologist and philosopher William James made an interesting observation. He said: "The greatest discovery of my generation is that human beings can alter their lives by altering their attitudes of mind."[1] He's right, because the truth is: What we focus on grows. Family and affirming friends can play a big part in helping us keep a positive attitude and stay centered on what's good, right and true. Then, as we focus on worthwhile endeavors and persevere through the challenges, we usually become better people. Our attitudes DO alter our lives.

One of my modern-day heroes is Lieutenant Scott Smiley, who was blinded by an explosion during combat in Iraq. Upon learning his blindness was permanent, the West Point graduate was tempted (as any of us might be) to think that the only future worth having was gone. But with the encouragement of his wife, Tiffany, and his close friends, he realized he still had many God-given gifts and abilities. One of them was teaching. So he enrolled in an MBA program at Duke University and lined up a teaching position at West Point, training new recruits upon his 2009 graduation. Not surprisingly, in 2007 Lieutenant Smiley was named Soldier of the Year.[2]

Scott Smiley found a new purpose greater than himself. My mother certainly recognized a purpose greater than herself. Purpose kept both of them going, it stretched them, and ultimately others around them benefited. Even though my mom didn't live long enough to see the fruit of her labor in her sons' lives, she had the comfort of knowing she was making the best use of the time she had. Rick Warren, pastor and author of The Purpose Driven Life, agrees that "Living with purpose is the only way to **really** live."[3]

Questions to Ponder:

What is your "why" your purpose beyond yourself?

What are you doing to ensure that you fulfill this purpose?

How are you stretching yourself in order to improve?

ROUND FOUR
Decisions and Defining Moments

"The most important goal for my children and their planning is that their college education be fully funded."

Janet Fishman Newman

Most great coaches and teachers will tell us that the first step toward improving our future is paying attention when our minds envision significant possibilities and solutions. The next step is even more important; acting on those worthy insights and solutions. We all have moments when a good and right idea becomes crystal clear to us. Those are the defining moments that can direct our paths if we follow up with good decisions and steadfast actions. Thankfully, my mom was a possibility thinker who took action on a number of wise decisions.

One such decision was a financial action she took that made a huge difference for Andrew and me. Long before she got sick, my mother began thinking about the future, and she purchased a $100,000.00 term life insurance policy to ensure that there would be tuition funding for Andrew and me when we were ready for college. Because of her vision and planning, I was able to attend Michigan State University and complete my degree without college loans. Andrew was able to attend Syracuse University in New York, fully funded as well. The opportunity to receive an education is an incomparable benefit. However, her gift also provided a further advantage for me. It led to a personal revelation, a defining moment and a meaningful decision in my life.

This is what happened: My father came to visit me at Michigan State during the early months of my freshman year. He invited me and a friend to have dinner at a nice restaurant in East Lansing, Michigan. Over dessert, my dad looked across the table at me and said, "Ben, what is it you want to do with your life?" Until that moment, I had not consciously determined the answer to this question. However, when he asked it, I found myself saying that I wanted to sell life insurance. As the words came out of my mouth, I realized they were true. I wanted to help others protect their families and prepare for the future the way our mother had provided for me and Andrew.

I was surprised that my father was not happy with this answer. In fact, if memory serves me correctly, he pounded his fist on the table and said, "No son of mine will go to college to have a career selling life insurance!" Throughout my life, I had longed for his approval and had tried to do things I thought he would respect. So it was difficult to hear his negative response, a response that shut down any discussion of the personal vision that felt important to me and would continue to be important. I didn't know it at the time, but my own brief verbal expression of this dream was a defining moment.

Because of my father's strong opinion and my need for

his approval, however, I tried other types of work during my college years. One job was at a mortgage company that sold what I now realize were sub-prime loans. At the time, I was just a hungry college kid looking for a couple of bucks to get by. It took a while for me to realize that I was not merely helping people secure loans, I was facilitating second mortgages for people who had no business refinancing.

By the time I fully understood this, I was finishing college and running a telemarketing center for this same mortgage company. When I graduated, my manager offered me a position in Troy, Michigan, making an annual salary of $100,000. In 2001, a $100,000 salary was very enticing to a 22-year-old. I remember he complimented my achievements and told me I'd be great for the Troy opportunity. Again, though, I surprised myself by speaking something that was bubbling up inside me. I told my boss I couldn't take the job because I no longer believed in the company or its policies. This was another defining moment for me; this time with a decision involving ethics. I realized that I could not encourage people to do something that was not in their best interest. This experience helped me understand that making good ethical decisions is more important to me than making a higher income.

Another defining moment occurred near the time of college graduation. My father contacted me, and said he wanted me to study for the LSAT, go to law school, and then come home to St. Louis and work in his law practice. I appreciated his offer, but at that moment I knew I couldn't accept it. My decision came fairly quickly. I remember telling him, "Dad, I'm thankful for the opportunity you're offering me, but I'm going to make a life of my own. I'm not going to go to law school. I'm going into sales. And

I'm going into sales because I believe I have the ability to build strong relationships with people and make a significant difference in the world by helping them find what they need."

My father's reaction was quiet; he seemed almost mystified. He wondered how I could turn down such profitable work and the opportunity to help build his practice with him. Additionally, I think he feared that a career in sales could lead to a career in life insurance. I may never know what he actually thought that day. But the lesson I learned was to trust my instincts and to make decisions for myself. Seeking input and feedback from others is important, but I believe we must make our own decisions.

Although I didn't know exactly where I would land, I somehow knew I had found my calling, and I had to stand and reach for it. But I did so with considerable disquietude. At the time, I probably would have been encouraged by the wisdom of business philosopher Jim Rohn, who said: "Let the views of others educate and inform you, but let your decisions be a product of your own conclusions."[1]

Undoubtedly, the two most significant defining moments in my adult life were when I met Ami and when J. Isaac was born. Ami is an incredible woman, a model of strength for many who know her. Her love and influence make me better every day.

I clearly remember the momentous Thursday afternoon of our meeting. We were both working out at Wellbridge Athletic Club in St. Louis. I was there with my buddy, Brett Cherry, who is a wonderful catalyst for making fun things happen. As we were lifting weights, he noticed Ami across the gym. Brett and Ami were already acquaintances and saw each other regularly at the gym. (I had seen her a few times before and always thought she was a real knock out.) Brett decided to head over in Ami's direction to catch up.

They talked about Brett's children and Brett commented that Ami needed children. She was quick to point out that step one was to meet her future husband. Once Brett learned that she was single, he walked with Ami in my direction and said, "Oh, so you're single? Well my buddy Ben Newman is single, too!" I remember my cheeks getting a little red as I said hello. Ami also blushed and giggled. Somewhat embarrassed, we each went back to our workouts. Brett then dared me to ask Ami for her phone number. I always liked a good challenge, so I took Brett up on his dare. I'm glad I did, and I'm glad Ami gave me her number that day. Following up on the commitment I made to call her was the best decision of my life. A couple years later, on Nov 11, 2006, my life took a magnificent turn when Ami became my wife.

After eighteen incredible months of marriage, Ami and I experienced a new defining moment, our son J. Isaac (his legal name is the letter "J" named after my mother), was born on March 4, 2008. I quickly discovered that the heavy responsibility of parenting is nevertheless a remarkable one. However, because of my mother and how she lived her life, I felt I had many valuable lessons to share. For starters, I made the decision to cherish the time I have with Ami and J. Isaac. I try not to rush the moments we have together in the mornings before I go to work, and I enjoy keeping my commitment to be home by 5:30 each weekday. Being present and focused with Ami and Isaac makes every day more worthwhile.

****

When I think about the conclusions each of us reach during our defining moments, several principles come to mind that help us make the decisions necessary to implement those conclusions. There's nothing original about these ideas; they're pretty basic. But I've noticed that people who follow them usually live their lives in a fairly admirable, productive way.

The first principle is: **Be resourceful**! I read an article in the "Chicago Tribune" years ago that remains with me. In fact, I have a quotation from it on my desk that reads: "Contrary to what you've heard, opportunity does not knock. You knock and opportunity answers." Those words encourage resourcefulness in me. In fact, they remind me not to wait for "BIG" opportunities but, rather, to take common occasions and use them wisely.

The second principle is: **Surround yourself with great people and learn from them.** Few things compare to the influence our associates can have on us. We may be pursuing an endeavor that is new to us, so having good and wise people around us quickens our pace of progress on the learning curve. In fact, Jim Rohn said, "Don't join an easy crowd. You won't grow. Go where expectations and demands are high."[2] How right he is!

The third principle that follows closely behind is: **Set wise standards.** When we put good policies in place in our lives, it simplifies some of our daily decisions. I have several policies I try to follow consistently. For example, with regard to our personal finances, Ami and I make it a practice to save 20 percent and donate at least 10 percent. I also try to leave each situation better than I found it and live so that clients and friends can trust my confidentiality and advice. These personal standards often simplify life for me.

The fourth principle is: **Create a plan.** My mother had a vision for her sons' college educations, and she put a plan in place. Along those same lines, but with very different results, my grandfather confided to me on his deathbed that he wished he'd created a savings plan to set aside money for his loved ones. He'd earned a nice income over the years but had not invested resources so he could leave a financial legacy for his children and grandchildren. None of us were expecting an inheritance, but he deeply regretted that he did not have one to give. He wished he'd created a plan.

We all have moments that seem to set us on a new path or "define" the future in a way we hadn't previously understood. It's wise to pay attention to the insights gleaned at those times and to follow through with appropriate decisions and actions. As we do, the principles I've outlined above may be helpful in the process of stepping forward onto an unfamiliar path.

Question to Ponder:

What defining moments in your life have revealed your inner desires in sharper focus?

What principles have provided wise "guardrails" as you embarked on a new endeavor?

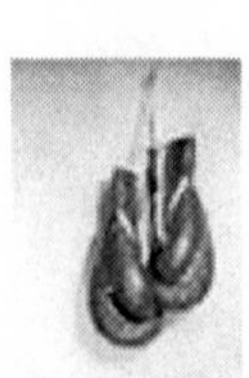

ROUND FIVE
Courage in Pursuit of Capacity

"Anita gave me a pamphlet on the most asked questions about amyloidosis. When I got to life expectancy, I was really upset. I called Anita and she came. We talked and I felt better, but for the first time, I saw in writing that hoping for 10 years is pushing it. However, I'm hopeful that with continued research and my will to live, I'll beat the statistics."

Janet Fishman Newman

None of us know how many years we will have on this earth. Nor can we anticipate the course of the future or estimate the capacity of our own bodies. When we are young and time seems to stretch out unendingly, we don't give much thought to these unknowns. However, as adults considering the brevity of life, we are challenged to think about our personal capacity and our legacy. My mother passionately wanted to push beyond statistical limits to reach her full capacity. My mother's passion to live as long as possible and do as much good as possible motivates me to make each day count. I know my mom fervently wanted more years to live, love and serve others.

Her shortened opportunity inspires me to be intentional about redeeming the time that *I* have. When I started in my current profession as a life insurance salesman, the local office was in downtown St. Louis was not a convenient drive from my home. In an effort to save time, money and gas, I worked at home many days. I made a conscious choice during work-day hours to keep the TV turned off, to stay "on task" from 8 to 5 and to never take naps.

As a single guy, I also took advantage of my free time to make evening appointments whenever I could. In those first years, I sometimes worked until 10 pm. Knowing I would be married someday, I wanted to put in the long hours that building my business required, so I would not be taking time away from a wife and children in the future. It was a sacrifice that led to my most prized possession today; time with family. I feel richly blessed that each day I am able to be home by 5:30 each evening with Ami and Isaac. What I have learned from this is that we usually have to make sacrifices in life to eventually enjoy the freedoms that are most important.

We've all heard that the average person uses only about 10 percent of his or her potential, which leaves 90% of our potential untapped. This fact emphasizes the axiom that there's always room to grow. We may think we just don't have any more energy, ideas, patience, vision, enthusiasm, determination or talent. And that may be true — for the moment. We may dearly need a good meal or a good night's sleep. But once we are refreshed, the truth is we probably *do* have room to grow. We don't need to expect great things of ourselves overnight. We simply need to be thoughtful about our capacity and be willing to stretch. Sometimes I think we overestimate what we can do in a month or a year, but we greatly underestimate the fruit of five or six years of strategic discipline. I found myself nodding enthusiastically when I recently read these words by Ben Franklin:, "Be not afraid of growing too slowly. Be afraid only of standing still."[1]

Reaching for our capacity does take discipline and courage. It's not easy to forge into a new arena or replace a bad habit with a healthy one. Over the years, I've come to see several truths that help me plod ahead.

The first is simple. I try to **look at every problem as an opportunity to learn and grow**. An unexpected challenge can be the very stimulus that inspires creativity and outside-the-box thinking. Such a challenge can also provide exercise for mental and emotional muscles we hadn't previously used. If we face our obstacles and don't try to ignore them, our personal capacity grows.

This definitely happened to Ami and me when we were newlyweds. Less than one month after our wedding, the health of my maternal grandparents took a turn for the worse, and Ami and I became primary caregivers for my grandparents. Their health had deteriorated to the point that we needed to do their grocery shopping every Sunday, take care of routine errands and, eventually, visit the nursing home and hospital every night after leaving work. It was difficult to keep up with our two busy careers as all this was going on. At times we couldn't help but think, "we're to young to be doing this." But with God's help we redoubled our efforts at discipline and scheduling and managed to remain professionally productive, as well. In fact, the most intense months of family care-giving were coincidently some of the most successful months for my business that year, due in part to earlier disciplines created. So Ami and I were honored to be able to be available for my grandparents, and we got the unexpected blessing of being stretched and strengthened in personal capacity.

Another thing that encourages me when I'm facing obstacles is the principle of minimization. I try to **analyze the challenge and break it down into small, do-able pieces.** Acclaimed Olympic gold medalist Michael Phelps is an inspiration to many in the versatility and magnitude of what he accomplished. Phelps won eight gold medals in the 2008 Summer Olympics in Beijing. For 36 years, the Olympic record in gold-medal swimming competitions (seven gold medals) had been held by Mark Spitz, who swam two strokes (freestyle and butterfly) at a maximum of 200 meters. Michael Phelps had a far greater challenge, swimming all four strokes (butterfly, freestyle, breast and back) for a maximum distance of 400 meters. Competing in 17 races over a period of nine days, Phelps had to deal with the combined challenge of exhaustion and versatility. However, he and his coaches had prepared for such challenges in training, breaking down the factors of preparation into manageable daily and weekly exercises. [2]

It's amazing how the seemingly impossible can become possible when we analyze our challenges and divide them into daily disciplines. It's equally amazing how maintaining such discipline increases our personal capacity.

Stretching to be our best, however, does not protect us from discouraging remarks or outright criticism. I will discuss in a later chapter the value of accepting feedback. However, I want to say here that it is important to try to assess the source of the feedback. Is it coming from an advocate or an adversary? I'm coming to understand that it's important for me to question where I am spending my time. Am I spending it with the adversaries who tell me that my ideas aren't possible and my goals are too big? Or am I spending more time with the individuals who challenge me daily to grow, who care about me and support my vision and dreams? Because I know what's most helpful for me, I encourage others to invest time in their advocate relationships. I believe that doing this increases our probability of success and happiness in life.

So I try to consciously put a third principle into play. I determine to **be bold and persevere in spite of rejection or the threat of failure**. In this resolve, I'm encouraged by a heartfelt comment former Prime Minister of Israel, Golda Meir, once made. She told a journalist, "I can honestly say that I was never affected by the question of the success of an undertaking. If I felt it was the right thing to do, I was for it, regardless of the possible outcome."[3] What better way to have courage for persevering than to base our decisions on what is good, right and true! Then we can let go of anxiety over results or public opinion and focus on staying true to the course we have set.

When Ami and I watched our son Isaac learning to crawl, we noticed that no outside influences seemed to prevent him from getting back up time and time again to achieve his goal of getting to a toy. A baby's pure determination is fascinating, because there is no fear of failure, rejection or discomfort. I want to keep a child-like mindset that doesn't allow discomfort or fear to hinder my progress. Post-modern adult thinking is full of "doom and gloom," in part due to some very real concerns: war, economic pressures and natural disasters. So I need to constantly remind myself of this truth: Individuals make a difference, goals matter, minds and attitudes are powerful forces.

Experience shows that the decisions and choices we make on a daily basis determine where we wind up in the world. I think that's why Thomas Edison claimed, "If we all did the things we are capable of doing, we would literally astound ourselves."[4]

My mother dreamed of beating the odds and outliving medical probabilities. She didn't want any of her life's potential to go unused. Her drive inspires me to make sure I live life to the fullest and tap as much of my God-given potential as possible. And so I share this challenge with you: Look at your opportunities, face the obstacles in front of you and resolve to stretch and reach for all you can be.

Questions to ponder:

What obstacles seem to be holding you back right now?

What areas of your life might be in need of stretching and growth?

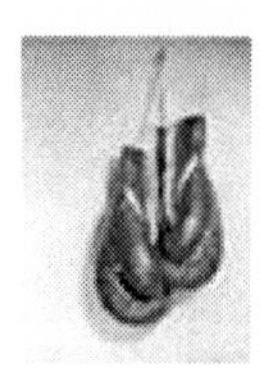

ROUND SIX
Help

"I discussed my fears with Mom and Steve and Derry, who were here and very supportive and encouraging. Then I felt better."

Janet Fishman Newman

British author George Eliot once said, "What do we live for, if it is not to make life less difficult for each other."[1] My mother was much admired for the love, energy and help she gave others. She was also smart enough to receive help when she needed it and to show gratitude. Her journal is full of anecdotes praising family, friends and hospital staff for their acts of thoughtfulness. As I mentioned earlier, she loved to record names of favorite hospital personnel and information about their families, so she could inquire and converse in a caring way during procedures. She was intensely interested in others.

I'm not sure if I unconsciously learned this from my mom when I was young, but I too, have a burning passion for helping others. I'm particularly enthusiastic about helping people discover their vision and empowering them as they create a larger future for themselves. It's actually what led me to choose the financial-security business I'm in today.

Before my first public-speaking engagement to a group of life insurance professionals, I developed an acronym for the word HELP. The word is so important to me, I could picture it written across a large whiteboard, with each letter standing out. The "H" in this acronym stands for "habits." Our habits are the incredibly important things that determine where we go in life. We may be born with certain advantages, but we become champions only when we apply good habits. Similarly, we can minimize our weaknesses with strategically formed habits.

When I began my life insurance career, the managing partner at our office, John Qualy (whom I very much admire), told me that if I built the habit to see 15 people each week, I would experience success in the business. If I met with 20 people per week, I would go beyond success to significance in what I could earn and in what I could do for others. When I left his office that day, it was as if he had never mentioned the number 15. I knew I would work to keep 20 appointments a week, not so much for the personal income as for the opportunity to impact other people's lives. Now a seasoned veteran in the business, I keep that same discipline today.

One of the other habits I try to follow is doing my best for a client and not giving up. For example, when a client's policy application is declined, I go back to the underwriter again and again to submit helpful information and more detailed medical files. I want to be the kind of person who never stops fighting for my clients or their dreams. "H" is for Habits. If I want to help others, I need to have good habits.

"E" is for "Expectations." In our personal and professional lives, clear expectations are the best predictor of worthy accomplishments. In fact, the more clearly we can define our hopes for the future, the more likely we'll be to: ask the questions, set the goals, develop the habits and make the strategic moves that lead us to the outcome we desire.

My friend Roland Williams tells a story of his dad's expectation for him that went far beyond his own vision. It started the summer before Roland's senior year in high school, when his father learned about a football camp at nearby Syracuse University. Though Roland loved playing high school football, he was not particularly interested in attending the camp with kids from places he'd never been. But what his dad knew that Roland didn't know was that this camp was where top players in the country were scouted by Syracuse and other universities, schools with potential scholarships. So, to encourage Roland's attendance, his father simply told him, "I just want you to go and do your best at the game you love."

An obedient son, Roland attended the camp, arriving with all his belongings in a trash bag because he didn't own a suitcase. He was committed to playing his best to honor his dad's expectation of him, unaware that his performance could impact his future. Several days into the camp, he called his father and explained that all the "big time recruits" attending the camp weren't really that good. It was because he beat them so easily that he thought they weren't good. But his dad redefined his expectations for his own life. He convinced Roland that it wasn't that the others weren't good, it was that HE WAS SO GOOD! This monumental lesson helped Roland set his own expectations high, and helped him realize that his best was good enough! Roland Williams' overall performance turned out to be one of the best at the camp that year. As a result, he earned a full scholarship to Syracuse University, from which he later spring-boarded into the NFL.

Obviously Roland has great talent, but his eight-year NFL career, Super Bowl championship with the St. Louis Rams and subsequent charitable work might not have been possible without his father's vision, sacrifice and wise expectations. Experience shows that healthy expectations are of great importance as we grow personally and as we help others. "Healthy expectations" is an important distinction to consider. If Roland had not had athletic talent, all the scouting camps in the world would not have helped him. If football had been Roland's father's dream but not Roland's, the expectations would have been unhealthy. We can't live other people's dreams for them or follow expectations that are wrong for our talents. But healthy and right expectations help us pursue excellence.

The "L" in my HELP acronym stands for "Lead to." Our good habits and wise expectations lead to something very valuable. They lead to Performance, the last element in my acronym. If a person has good daily habits and healthy expectations, these will almost invariably lead to an admirable performance.

When I finished my career-training class, I wrote a personal goal across the top of my monthly tracking report. My personal expectation was to build a practice with the elite of the company. I was a fresh recruit who hadn't sold a single policy, yet I wanted to be among the most seasoned professionals in the company! My associates in our monthly accountability group — and even my managing partner — said I needed to be more realistic. But I stuck with the original (and larger) goal. And I believe the larger goal pushed me to do more than I otherwise would have done. I didn't see the fruit of my work immediately, but in the fourth year, I became a member of a prestigious group of the top 2 percent of financial representatives in our company. In addition, that same year I was among only a handful of individuals to accomplish the goal while still in my 20's. I'm glad I had the courage to stand up to those who said my goal was too big.

One of the things I learned from that experience is this: We don't have to wait to be successful. Yes, I may have been overly aggressive, but length of service doesn't matter as much as great expectations and habits. Over and over again, the HELP acronym proves valid: **Habits + Expectations Lead to Performance.**

And the truth is, productivity in performance increases our ability to help others. When we're productive, we often have more resources with which to lend a helping hand. These resources might involve sharing information, offering personal encouragement, making valuable networking introductions or occasionally even arranging financial help. The help we most often give others, though, does not involve herculean effort, but rather some resource at our fingertips that we can easily offer.

Most people say that nothing makes them feel better than helping others. I agree, and I'm inspired by a statement Scottish novelist Compton MacKenzie made years ago. He said, "If I were a godfather wishing a gift on a child, it would be that he should always be more interested in other people than in himself."[2] This trait of being other-centered is something Ami and I deeply desire to pass on to our son. This is important to me because it is part of my mom's legacy that I feel honored to be able to pass down our family tree.

I recently had the opportunity to spend time with one

of my mother's former students, Eldad Bialecki. Eldad recalled how much my mom seemed to love teaching and being with her students. He claimed that her care for students seemed much deeper than that of any other teacher he had in his life, and he was greatly influenced by her. Such stories about my mother are commonplace when I talk to her former students. They are a sweet affirmation of my mother's character. And hearing them talk about her provides yet another opportunity for me to understand more of who she was, in addition to being my mother.

Though my goal is not self-serving, I've discovered a somewhat surprising by-product of caring for others: We often receive a double blessing in return. First, we get the benefit of knowing we made a difference for someone else. And that can really make our day! However, additional blessing frequently comes our way because, as John Maxwell explains in his book, The 360-Degree Leader, "people always move toward someone who increases them and away from anyone who decreases them."[3] So the practice of adding value to others usually brings favor back to us.

Question to Ponder:

What habit or expectation could you change today that might increase your effectiveness in helping others?

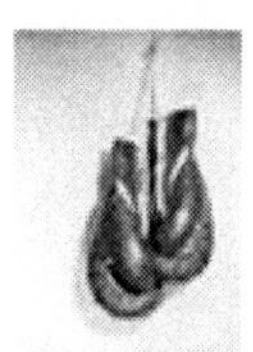

ROUND SEVEN
Embrace the Adversity

"I believe...[I] will pull...through as long as I keep working at it, where maybe someone else would succumb to it. I just want to grow old with my kids and enjoy their futures."

Janet Fishman Newman

I am inspired by my mother's tenacity. Nowhere in her journal do I find any sign of self-pity or bitterness over her circumstances. Nor is there a hint of denial. She seems to have embraced the challenge of battling amyloidosis while looking for the joy in life and living each day to the fullest. A lesser person might have given into resentful 'why me?' questions, becoming peevish or ill-tempered. Someone else battling such an imposing disease might have given up on the discipline of trying to make the most of each day. I'm proud of my mother's legacy of perseverance.

One journal entry details an experience my mother had with a resident at Barnes-Jewish Hospital in St. Louis, Missouri. She wrote, "the resident came back and said as he pushed on my chest, '[this] must not hurt too bad because you aren't complaining.' I told him I was a lot perturbed ... and not to judge.... 'I don't complain but take my word for it; it hurts. Pain is relative.'" It is remarkable to me that, faced with situation when screaming and complaining would have been acceptable, my mother fought the negativity. She seemed to always find strength to deal with her obstacles. She believed what I so strongly believe today: Our biggest obstacles mask our greatest opportunities.

A number of years ago, Ann Landers shared some very wise advice. She wrote: "If I were asked to give what I consider the single most useful bit of advice for all humanity, it would be this: Expect trouble as an inevitable part of life, and when it comes, hold your head high, look it squarely in the eye and say, 'I will be bigger than you. You cannot defeat me'."[1] Landers is right. Trouble is an inevitable part of life. Though we live in a culture that sometimes seems to favor denial and avoiding responsibility, we can't actually escape adversity. And we gain strength by facing obstacles. Every worthwhile endeavor in life — education, marriage, childrearing, career achievement — involves challenges.

It may be a natural part of the human psyche to want to hide. As a salesman, I have moments when I want to run from the challenge of dealing with cold calls, broken appointments or negative underwriting decisions, but I've trained my mind to remember that these feelings don't last. I don't hide under an emotional rock. Instead, I might call my wife to vent for a few minutes, but then I will get right back to the problem at hand.

As a father, when I'm awakened for the fourth time in one night, it's tempting to pull the covers over my head and turn off the baby monitor. But again, the discouraging feelings don't last. As I comfort our baby boy and watch him quickly fall back to sleep, or when I see his infectious smile in the morning, I am reminded that it is all worth it.

Business consultants and life coaches tell us a good way to face an obstacle is to look for a positive outcome we can work toward. My friend John O'Leary shares a great story of being encouraged to work toward a positive outcome. When John was 9 years old, he was burned on nearly 100 percent of his body and given less than a 1 percent chance of surviving the first night. He did survive and endured months in the hospital, dozens of surgeries and lost all his fingers to amputation.

One day while he was in the hospital, Baseball Hall of Fame sports announcer Jack Buck surprised John with a visit. During their conversation, the excited 9 year old asked Jack if he could get him a baseball signed by Ozzie Smith. Jack fulfilled the request several days later. Overjoyed, John asked for a baseball signed by another sports legend. Jack Buck wisely decided to challenge John. He told him he would get him another baseball, if John would write a thank-you note for the first one. It might have been a risky challenge, since John had only stubs for fingers, but Jack sensed young John would be motivated enough to accept the task. He did, and that was the beginning of a number of baseballs and a number of thank-you letters.

O'Leary, now an adult, looks back on that challenge as the beginning of his "yes I can" attitude. As a college graduate, business owner, philanthropist, husband and father, John O'Leary has an understandable passion for empowering others a passion that began with Jack Buck giving him a positive outcome to work toward. An interesting side note is that in 2006, the Energizer Corporation inducted John into its "Keep Going" hall of fame. In my mind, that's symbolic of the fact that working toward something positive keeps us going.

In his book, Rhinoceros Success, Scott Alexander invites the reader to picture himself as: "three tons of snorting rhinoceros charging full speed at your opportunity, mowing down all obstacles in your way."[2] Our St. Louis insurance practice shares Alexander's rhino mentality of charging over our fears with a reckless abandon. We try to think of it as charging toward the opportunities to help clients and to grow professionally. What is unique about our office is that we are in the small market of St. Louis, Missouri. Financial Representatives in larger cities have far more families and corporations with which to work in generating business. Yet representatives in our office don't use that as an excuse. We use it as motivation to prove that anything is possible. In 2008, our office achieved the highest volume in sales in the entire country for our company. We feel our record proves that belief in one's purpose drives results, and our purpose is protecting lives and making an impact on our client's families.

A focus on purpose and a positive mental attitude like my mother's are great tools for dealing with obstacles. Another helpful way to manage adversity involves having the courage to share problems with friends. In Round Four, I mentioned the value of surrounding ourselves with good people and learning from them. As we turn to friends for counsel in adversity, it becomes clear how important it is to associate with men and women who have good values, who listen, who possess sound reasoning and who care enough to tell us the truth. None of us is perfect. We can always do better. If we're open to feedback, we'll most certainly become stronger and wiser.

A popular piece of wisdom in the world of mentoring and coaching is that "feedback is the breakfast of champions."

We each have friends who care about us and who notice important details in our lives. Since we do not have 360-degree vision, we can receive great value from letting safe friends and relatives know that we are open to feedback and will not become defensive.

In addition to the surrogate parents God gave me over the years, my best friends Josh and Andy have been the kind of buddies with whom I could discuss anything. Nothing has been so embarrassing or difficult that it was off limits. And their insights have always helped broaden or deepen my perspective. I think one of the strongest temptations in life is to hold back from sharing our thoughts and our emotions with others when we need help. Yet experience has taught me that there's great value in being honest and transparent in my relationships. I compare it to someone going to the doctor with significant pain, but not telling the doctor all the symptoms. The physician's help cannot be complete without the full story. I sense that it was very tough for my mother to endure all her procedures and tests, yet they led to a correct diagnosis and to some extra months of life for her. Had she given up on allowing others to help her, I may not have had the last beautiful year I had with my mother.

I have been blessed with so many loving family members and friends in my life. I believe the richness in those relationships can be traced back to trusting my mother's example of being honest and transparent with others, allowing their help.

Perhaps a third way to successfully embrace adversity is to read good books. It's true that we become what we feed our minds. So it's wise to be particular about what we read, what we watch and what we listen to. Scott Alexander advises that before we spend time on a form of education, we should ask ourselves, "Will the information in this book help me reach my goals?"[3] Of course, reading can be just for enjoyment, too, but when we're wanting to grow, it's wise to be discerning in our choices.

Several books that have particularly encouraged me during times of challenge are: The Energy Bus by Jon Gordon, Be All You Can Be by John Maxwell, and The Strangest Secret by Earl Nightingale. Another great book is The Winner's Manual for the Game of Life. In it, Ohio State University coach Jim Tressel claims, "If our attitude is one that embraces learning and growing, we'll treat adversity as a stepping stone … rather than … as an insurmountable obstacle. But if we have a negative attitude and become defensive at the first hint of criticism or begin to blame others for our mistakes, we'll miss the opportunity to develop into the types of people we want to be."[4]

When I find a book that particularly inspires me, I like to memorize meaningful quotes from it and incorporate them into my life when I can. I like to try to process information for inspirational change and growth.

One final way I try to embrace adversity is to consider the future. I ask myself how the decisions I make today will impact the future that I want for my wife and son. Looking at the current challenge from that perspective clears away the emotion of the moment and helps me move ahead.

Questions to ponder:

What's your most pressing adversity today?

What are some positive outcomes you can work toward within that challenge?

Who is in your network of supportive, honest friends? Do you need to deepen those relationships?

How will the decisions you make today impact your future?

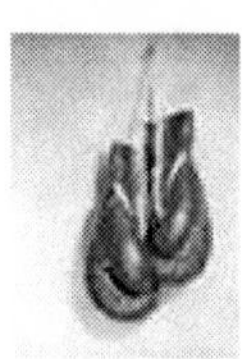

ROUND EIGHT
The Daily Fight

"I must assume responsibility for myself, change my lifestyle and alter my diet to live with this disease that is chronic and fatal, to beat the statistics, beat the odds, and live a long life with my kids."

Janet Fishman Newman

We each face a daily fight in our chosen endeavors and careers. For a young mother at home, the fight might be to remain patient in childcare; for a salesman, the fight might involve networking and intently listening to clients; for a teacher, the fight might entail ever more creative lesson planning and classroom management.

My mother's fight was about life and living. And, indeed, she saw it as a charge to fight for her life. I find her vision particularly interesting, because in her day the majority of people assumed that medical professionals had sole responsibility for finding solutions and dispensing medicine that would somehow make us healthy. The idea of being our own advocates, learning every detail about the most helpful diet, and taking responsibility for seeking alternative medical answers was not something people commonly considered at the time.

I get very emotional reading my mother's comments of resolve and bravery. I'm also touched by the list of positive phrases and self-motivating notes she recorded in her journal that would lift her when she was discouraged. She exhorted herself to: "beat the odds," "beat the statistics," "live with my kids," "laugh," "love, hope," accept "support," let go of "fear, depression, panic," have "confidence in self, believe in self," "assume responsibility for self, [for] lifestyle change, [and for] diet." She did everything she knew how to do, and her actions inspire me to persevere in my daily challenges, which often seem easy when compared to hers.

With her inspiration, I've spent time thinking about this concept of a daily fight. For most of us, I believe the "fight" can be broken down into smaller components that are easier to manage. My daily fight seems to be comprised of three principles.

The first principle of my daily fight is habitual action. I've often heard this axiom: "Confidence is contagious; lack of confidence is equally contagious, and a customer will recognize both."[1] Confidence doesn't develop in a vacuum. Football Hall of Fame quarterback Roger Staubach rightly maintains that confidence is "the result of something … hours and days and weeks and years of constant work and dedication."[2] So my clients need to be able to sense something of my preparation and proficiency as I contact and work with them. This means that without being arrogant, I want to demonstrate my knowledge in each interaction, though openly admitting it if I don't know something. Obviously, I want to "check my ego at the door" and be open to learning from other experts. However, my poise in listening, in gathering information and in giving clear confident explanations can reassure clients that the decisions and measures we take together are wise.

The second principle of my daily fight is accepting responsibility and not making excuses. Winston Churchill said, "The price of greatness is responsibility."[3] And it's true, we impact those around us most positively when we are accountable. I believe this applies to every individual, no matter the status or circumstance. We each have to assume responsibility for ourselves and for those who are dependent on us, whether it involves something daily like a regular workout to keep blood pressure down or putting in the hours to finish a promised project on time. I admire how my mom — weakened by disease — still took responsibility for researching her illness, changing doctors when necessary and altering her diet.

Admittedly, it's often difficult to accept responsibility and not make excuses. Occasionally, for example, I'll have a client call and ask me to take on a task that may cut into my productive time or my commissions, but one that is nevertheless a good and right thing to do. It would be easy to make excuses for why I could not follow through. However, I don't want to be an excuse-maker; I want to be an action-taker for those things that are reasonable and right for my clients and, of course, for my own family. I'm inspired by a comment Albert Einstein made: "A hundred times a day, I remind myself that my life depends on the labors of other men, living and dead, and that I must exert myself in order to give, in the measure as I have received."[4] Einstein obviously believed in the value of responsibility, too.

The third principle of my daily fight is what I call vitamin B. Vitamin B stands for belief. There are many things we each believe in that keep us strong. I believe in God and His promise to guide me when I am struggling on unfamiliar paths (Isaiah 42:16). With regard to my profession, I believe in the talents God gave me, the excellent training I've received, the trustworthy company I represent and the outstanding team with which I work. I believe in and rely on them. When I have done my homework and KNOW I am offering the best in product, information, tools and services, I approach clients and associates not simply with confidence, but with conviction and **belief.**

In the 2008 NBA finals, sports enthusiasts will recall that the Boston Celtics were down by an overwhelming 24 points against the Los Angeles Lakers in the second half of historic game four. The game looked all but lost for Boston. However, sportscasters replaying that game love to comment that Boston Coach Doc Rivers' passion and belief in his players noticeably intensified in the second half. I like to say that he was taking his vitamin B and encouraging his players with that belief, too. In the fourth quarter, the Celtics got to within 10 points of the Lakers' score and Doc Rivers began charging up and down the sidelines yelling, "Do you believe? Do you believe?" He was seemingly asking them: Do you believe you can win this? Do you believe in your training, in your teammates, in your program, in your talents enough to hang in there and persevere and give it your utmost every second for rest of this game? In what became the greatest comeback in NBA finals history, the Celtics went on to beat the Lakers that game. It was the defining moment in the series, which the Celtics won, 97 to 91, catapulting them to an NBA championship.

Obviously, simply believing something, doesn't on its own bring the desired results. Our beliefs have to be based on a solid foundation of truth; for example, an organization with integrity, a person of honor, a qualified program. And then we have to back up the conviction of our beliefs with wise, focused action.

Of course, it's also true that we can back up our well-founded beliefs with exceptional work and still not receive the desired result. However, the point I want to make is: It's sad to have the benefit of a solid foundation and not have the conviction or belief to stand up for it. I think that's what Doc Rivers was getting at in that now famous game four. He was saying, "are you convinced enough about the value of this program and the value of this team to stay in the game and do your best to win?" Habitual actions, responsible decisions, and well-founded beliefs: these are the principles that help me persevere in my daily fight. And we are all in our own daily fight. Sometimes it feels like we're just barely surviving. Other times, we have enough margin to really focus on giving it our best. Wherever you are on that continuum, I encourage you to understand the variables in your life and take satisfaction that you are doing your best to fight the good fight.

Questions to Ponder:

What are the principles of your daily fight?

Are you accepting responsibility for your actions in your life?

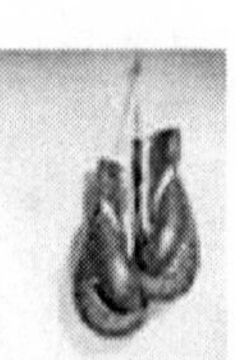

ROUND NINE
Mind's Eye

"Unfortunately, I had to have the right side of my heart catheterized, so again a risky procedure was at hand. The catheterization department and I recognized each other. Dr. Ali Salini and his team made me feel comfortable as we discussed crab rangoon, corned beef and the fact that the Cardinals were in the playoffs. I asked them ... was I going to get off the catheterization table without having to give up my playoff tickets? (I later made it to the game!)"

Janet Fishman Newman

My mom's desire to go to the St. Louis Cardinals playoff game is an endearing example of the value of plans, dreams and anticipation. Even though it was only a game, it promised to be an exciting one, and thinking about it seemed to give her energy and a determination that sustained her through another uncomfortable and somewhat risky procedure.

It's no secret that the things we set our minds on can encourage and sustain us through an uncomfortable time.

What's more, psychologists tell us that the things we hold in our mind's eye can actually be said to propel us in a given direction.

When I was young, one of the sports icons I followed was Muhammad Ali, a man with remarkable ability to picture athletic achievement in his mind's eye. My grandfather, Marcel, used to come over to the house and watch boxing with me, telling me all about the great fights and the great champions. We watched old fights and new ones, studying the moves of boxers like Ali and Frazier and Sonny Liston.

My grandfather told me that when Muhammad Ali (Cassius Clay) was a boy, he had his bike stolen and got beaten up on the streets several times. When he decided he had had enough, he determined that he would train in a gym and strengthen himself with boxing and other sports. People who remember Ali as scrawny 13-year-old Cassius Clay in Louisville, Kentucky, say that even as a youth, Clay began to envision great boxing achievements. He pictured the championship belt around his waist and referred to himself as the champion of the world.

Even before the earliest of his fights, he began telling people he was "the greatest." Many saw this as his attempt to psyche-out his opponents, but those who knew him well claim he believed his own self-proclaimed press. Certainly, over the years he got bruised, battered and knocked down in the ring. However, his professional record includes 62 fights; an amazing 57 of those fights were victories for Ali. He is a three-time World Heavy Weight Champion and an Olympic Gold Medalist who, in 1999, was named Sportsman of the Century by "Sports Illustrated." Muhammad Ali is a notable example of someone who held a vision in his mind's eye and let that vision propel him toward his dreams.

In my book Pocket Principles for the Insurance Business, I share 365 concepts that have helped me in the business world. Among them are: RAISE YOUR LEVEL OF CONSCIOUSNESS, SET BIG GOALS, SURPASS YOUR GOALS IN YOUR MIND'S EYE.

I firmly believe in the value of vision. A well-established mental picture can set an inner expectation that is so clear, we can do little other than follow it. What we hold in our mind's eye can diminish fear, distraction and even personal insecurities. However, we must devote energy to the development and maintenance of worthy pictures in our mind's eye. And we must take the steps necessary to fulfill the visions.

In her mind's eye, my mother envisioned my brother and me walking across the stage of our respective universities, receiving our diplomas. She felt the importance of that so clearly, she purchased the insurance to make it happen.

The entitlement society we live in sometimes distracts us from the responsibility of developing vision and taking the kind of action my mother did. We often find it difficult to pay or work for something today that offers a future benefit, but nothing immediate or tangible. Entitlements lull us into looking for security, when we would receive a bigger benefit from seeking freedom, instead.

Many people think that security and freedom are the same thing. I happen to believe that they are polar opposites. For example, in the culture in which I work, people know that our managing partner will pay the business' bills and keep the electricity turned on, whether or not individual company representatives faithfully complete their essential responsibilities. This is a form of security. However, if day after day, and week after week — because of that security

— the representatives did not complete their key strategic tasks, there would one day be no benefit for clients, no individual professional growth and no money for the company phones or electricity. So although security has value, it can also be the enemy of values which are greater, values like excellence, personal motivation and strategic thinking.

Because I work in a commission-based business, I've discovered that when I follow conscientious disciplines, use my God-given talents and focus on the needs of clients, I reach a level of professional success that allows personal freedom; freedom to spend time with my grandparents during the work day, for example, when they were ill, or freedom to take paternity leave when my son was born. Sometimes moving away from the secure life unlocks our personal potential and allows us to be productive rather than just active.

Most people I know would rather have a life where they've fought to make a difference, rather than one where they've merely settled for the status quo. A search for security usually leads to mediocrity, while focusing on excellence leads to freedom.

I believe the human psyche most longs to determine what we were made for, to choose our own dreams and then run after them. I'm humbled and blessed by the way my mother freely ran after her dream for me and my brother.

Several years ago, after a speech I had given in Woodland Hills, California, someone asked me, "What is your vision?" Because I have spent a lot of time thinking about this, it was easy to answer the question. I quickly listed my goals: to be in the top 2 percent of our company's sales force, to be an award-winning author and to be an internationally recognized motivational speaker. Through hard work and vision I achieved the first of those goals just prior to turning 30 years old.

Obviously, I don't want to put achievements before my time with family. They come first with me. Coming home is the true joy and blessing of my life. No matter how much success or rejection I have experienced during the day, Ami's warm welcome makes my day, just as my mother's welcome always did. They both demonstrate the true meaning of unconditional love. However, when I am in the middle of my work day, I believe it's very important to have vision and strategy for the direction I want to go. I work each day with immense focus and intensity.

The story is told that in 1895 some of Teddy Roosevelt's friends asked him if he would be a candidate for U.S. President. He reportedly said, "Don't you dare ask me that! Don't put such ideas into my head ... I won't let myself think of it ... because if I do, I will begin to work for it; I'll be careful, calculating, and cautious."[3]

Roosevelt seems to have agreed that what we can see in our mind's eye is what we begin to analyze and dwell on. If it seems worthy to us, our unconscious minds will set to work on it. As it turned out, Roosevelt actually ran successfully for the vice presidency several years later, after serving as assistant secretary of the Navy and subsequently governor of New York. In 1904, he ran for and was elected president.

His bid for the presidency was probably not so much due to the power of his friends' suggestions, as to his own leadership gifts and ability to envision worthwhile policy and needed reforms. His presidency includes a long list of visionary moves, but one that stands out in my mind is the Nobel Peace Prize he won in 1906 for mediating the end of the Russo-Japanese War.

As I offer examples of the visionary moves of Roosevelt and Ali and my mom, my purpose for this chapter is: to encourage you to look within, to rediscover your innate talents and to stretch your mind's eye for picturing the greatest personal potential possible.

Questions to Ponder:

Based on your talents, standards and values, what's worth setting your mind's eye on?

What steps do you want to take to bring your vision to life?

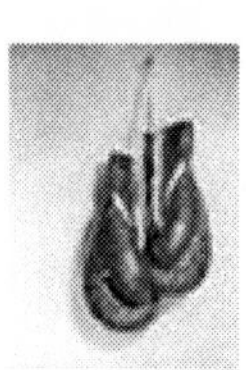

ROUND TEN
What Keeps You Up At Night?

"Anticipation of [these current] test results is very scary, because I can imagine the worst, knowing I've already been positively diagnosed [with amyloidosis] other places."

Janet Fishman Newman

My mother had long-term hopes and dreams that were threatened by the prognosis of disease. Worrying about the future probably kept her up more nights than did the very real physical pain she endured. Doctors can dispense medication for pain. And though she took pain medication very sparingly, my mother did take it. As she dealt with the pain, I'm sure there were nights she wondered if there was a remedy for worry.

Like my mom, everyone has hopes, dreams and goals of some kind. And everyone has circumstances that pose threats to those dreams. None of us can control what happens *to* us, but we can control what happens *within* us. We can manage our decisions, our behavior and our attitudes.

My mother faithfully took her medications, stuck to her diet and followed all the advised regimens for living with her illness. She was so good at maintaining positive attitudes and disciplines that after her death, her beloved physician, Dr. Martha Skinner, wrote the following comments in a letter to my grandparents:

Your daughter was a remarkable young woman. Her good cheer, courage to fight a dreadful condition, and ability to manage her life and family so capably are a lesson to us all. It is persons like Janet that keep us diligently working to find a better therapy for this disease.[1]

I can only imagine the complexities my mother encountered, balancing work and medical procedures with parenting two young boys, when she had so little energy. Her example of cheerful perseverance inspires me as I strive to reach important milestones in my adult life and as I coach others in doing so.

Even though success looks different for each person, I believe all men and women sincerely desire positive results in the important endeavors of their lives. However, most of us underestimate how much perseverance and discipline are required to reach for worthy goals.

I believe it's the act of reaching for our best and our family's best that can keep us up at night. And in my view, these occasional sleepless nights may be a positive force in our lives, because they prompt us to pray and to stay focused, and to find what good answers may be available. I read somewhere that Thomas Edison said, "I never did anything worth doing by accident, nor did any of my inventions come by accident. They came by work."[2] We never hear of someone "falling into" success. Solutions come through preparation, experience and hard work. We may not always get the result we were looking for, but we always get a far better result than if we did not plan, probe, and persevere.

In 2008, Ami and I had the opportunity to meet someone whose pressing nightly focus resulted in something extremely important in the medical field. Our meeting came about in the following way. I had been invited to speak to the leadership team at the Boston Medical Center as a result of my philanthropic work there. In making arrangements prior to the trip, I remembered a Dr. Skinner described fondly by my mother in her journal. So I contacted the hospital to see if Dr. Skinner was still there. Yes!, was the answer. Dr. Martha Skinner was not only there, but she was the head of the department for research of amyloidosis. And she remembered my mother well.

The trip became a meaningful opportunity to feel closer to my mother. When Ami and I visited with Dr. Skinner in her conference room, she told us it was the very conference room where she and my mother had conversed during those family trips to Boston so many years earlier. Additionally, Dr. Skinner still had the medical file folder with my mother's name handwritten on the label. Among other documents, the now 20-year-old folder contained the letter referenced earlier in this chapter, as well as a personal note from my grandfather praising Dr. Skinner for her compassion in working with my mother.

It was moving to speak with Dr. Skinner and realize that my mother had experienced the same conversational warmth and professional insight Ami and I were experiencing and in the same conference room. During the discussion, Dr. Skinner told us how sad she was that my mother had not lived ten years later. She explained that through continued research and unwavering perseverance, she and a team of physicians had discovered that chemotherapy can treat amyloidosis and can enable people to live with the disease!

Amyloidosis was obviously something that had kept Dr. Skinner up at night, as she thought about looking for life-extending solutions for her patients. I suspect it still keeps her up at night, as she searches for a complete cure. I was thrilled to hear of the successful treatment. But her revelation also took my breath away, as I thought of the missed possibilities for my mother. In fact, some people have told me they would have felt anger that it took so long to discover a therapy. My reaction was different, though. I was honored to be in the presence of the physician who worked so hard to find a therapy that would prevent other young children from experiencing what I did. Here was a woman who, like my mother, had an attitude that clearly shows perseverance, conviction and passion for a cause greater than herself.

So, occasional sleepless nights can be an advantage when they give us vision, focus and relentless endurance to work toward an important goal or milestone.

But perhaps a pertinent question to ask in the midst of pressing forward is this: How do we balance it all? It's a known fact that worry can be detrimental to our health; in fact, chronic worry can negatively impact our heart, glands, blood circulation and even our nervous system. How do we turn off worry and turn on creativity?

Several years ago, I took advantage of some sleepless nights to look at my life and determine what was causing unnecessary stress. It was a time of intense, personal honesty. Several issues kept resurfacing in those soul-searching hours, and they led me to a few helpful decisions. I discovered modifications that were within my control. As I saw positive steps I could take, I was able to begin to let go of worry, and a good measure of peace flowed in. Here are some of the things I saw I could do:

- Eliminate things in my schedule that did not add value
  to anyone.
- Determine ways to streamline several office procedures.
- Have courageous conversations when others placed unreasonable demands on me.

As I worked through these personal objectives, I realized that the first two involved careful insight and an intentional change of habits. Both could be somewhat challenging, but they were do-able with a little focus and self-discipline. The latter, however, involved thoughtful expression of perspective and securing agreement from others. This can be a little trickier.

One of my favorite books on this topic is The No Complaining Rule, written by my friend Jon Gordon. In compelling story format, Gordon illustrates positive ways to deal with negativity. At the outset, his characters are prone to whine and create a kind of cancer in the workplace with their complaints. Through a series of challenges, he shows the characters learning to analyze an issue and have courageous conversations with the appropriate decision maker in the situation.

Gordon suggests that in preparing for courageous conversations, it is valuable to refrain from complaining to others. It's also wise to decide how to positively state the crux of the issue, then to determine one or two viable solutions to the problem, and finally to make an appointment with a key person or persons who can help make necessary changes.

I have found these courageous conversations to

be effective in the workplace as well as in personal relationships. I share the concept here because I believe such conversations can be a valuable part of the solution for the kinds of things that keep most of us up at night. Courageous conversations certainly help me in coaching clients to follow through with the things they declare as their highest priorities.

Whatever your late-night worries may be, it is worth examining them for self discovery, revelation of truth and refocus. It might also be a great time for prayer, for asking God to lend His insight and guidance. I'm often reminded of what Abraham Lincoln said: "God is the silent partner in all great enterprises."[4] No one knows the depth of our problems or how they affect the future like God does. And no one can give counsel and guidance like He can (Psalm 32:8).

When positive resolutions suggest themselves after meditating on a problem, I try to think them through, weigh their value and determine which ones are best. Then I do the ONLY reasonable thing — I discipline myself to take the practical steps at hand.

So, when something keeps me up at night, I try to view it as an opportunity to grow professionally or personally. A small entry in my mother's journal seems to indicate she viewed it this way, too. Lying in a hospital bed late one December night, she wrote: "fear of the unknown can help motivate you, if [you don't let it become] debilitating."

Turning fear or worry into motivation is really about seeing the future with hope. When I say 'hope,' I'm not talking about vain imaginings, but about realistic dreams turned into practical steps. When Ohio State University Coach Jim Tressel talks about wanting to instill perseverance and courage in his team members, he says:

"The type of hope I want to instill in my players is proactive and based on reality, not on fantasy and wishful thinking. It's not the kind of hope a person might have when buying a lottery ticket with the last of the grocery money. Instead it's a constant belief in the work that's already been done, the planning that's in place, and the potential that lies ahead."5

When we know we're doing our best to prepare for tomorrow and to care for our families, there's a security that invites peaceful sleep.

Question to Ponder:

What keeps you up at night and what are you doing about it?

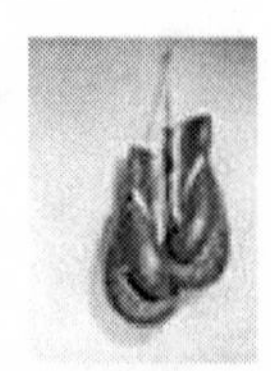

ROUND ELEVEN
You are Never Alone

"My Mother's notes are a gift. She did not have the opportunity to finish her journal, but her words have helped me find peace amidst obstacles and find hope for the future."

B.A. Newman

In late 2007, I was speaking at a planning meeting in Cincinnati, Ohio. Approximately 75 sales associates were gathered to brainstorm and set goals for the following year. My job was to encourage them in setting excellent goals and in persevering toward their objectives. For inspiration, I read aloud several excerpts from my mother's journal, interspersing these passages with truths I was learning in my own life about the value of pressing on in the face of obstacles.

After the meeting, my friend Ron Beshear approached me regarding my mother's journal. He commented on how interesting it was that 20 years after her death, I was inspiring others with the notes she kept during her terminal illness. He noticed how much her words seemed to move those in the audience that day. "She had so much courage in the face of obstacles, it inspires all of us," he said. "Maybe your mother's journal is a not only a gift to you, but also to the world. Perhaps it signifies that her work is not done yet."

Ron's comments reflect what others have suggested, too. It would be easy to think my mother's story ended on November 2, 1986. But her struggles had purpose, and amyloidosis was not the ultimate victor. My mother lived 38 beautiful years. She was an educator, a faithful friend, a devoted daughter, a loving sister and an amazing mother. Amyloidosis cannot take who she was nor what her life was about. Nor can it take away the fact that her hope and resolve often encourage others. In his book, The Purpose Driven Life, Pastor Rick Warren wisely commented, "What matters is not the *duration* of your life, but the *donation* of it." [1]

My mother was a huge giver! She gave time, energy and enthusiasm to everyone in her circle. Recently, I was contacted by a former student who had the benefit of being in my mother's second- and later her fourth-grade class. This gentleman, Jonathon Shanker, now a successful orthodontist in St. Louis, told me about how my mother had supported and nurtured him after his own mother died when he was in second grade. He told me of the difference she made in his life and the passion she had for helping others.

One particularly emotional memory was an experience Jonathan had with my mother during a timeout he had received from another teacher. Similar to how I struggled with my emotions after losing my mother, Jonathan had difficulty with his behavior. He often acted out, and with one teacher in particular he couldn't seem to stay out of trouble. As a result of his behavior in this gentleman's class, Jonathan was never allowed to attend recess.

One day, as he was pacing in the hallway while the others kids enjoyed playtime outside, my mother spotted him. She asked, "Why aren't you at recess with all the other kids." Jonathan explained that he never went to recess because of his behavior. What is unique about this story is that my mother took up his cause. She was furious that a child who had a legitimate grief in his life would be held back from a needed time of play at recess. Evidently, she went straight to the principal's office and stressed her opinion that the punishment was inappropriate. The principal agreed, Jonathan received vindication, and he was reunited with his friends.

I am blessed by my mother's example of taking the time to understand others and their feelings. Obviously, my brother and I received wonderful infusions of her energy and warmth every day. She showed us how to persevere and even celebrate life in the face of obstacles.

I still smile, remembering the day she brought home lobster for dinner. She'd had several weeks of struggling with pain down her arms and legs, and decided we needed to have a family party, no matter how she was feeling. So she purchased three live lobsters. Before cooking them, she invited us each to pick one and give it a name. Then we held several races across the kitchen floor to see whose lobster was the fastest. I remember my mother on the floor with me and Andrew, cheering just as boisterously for her lobster as we boys we're cheering for ours. Even though I knew my mother was sick, I don't remember our household being a sad, maudlin place. Her positive outlook brightened our home.

So even though she passed from this earth in 1986, her

legacy continues to impact me. What helped me see her legacy even more clearly was an industry meeting I attended in February, 2008. There, my friend Chris Koon introduced me to Jon Gordon, who wrote the foreword for this book. At the meeting, Gordon shared principles from his publication, The Energy Bus, a book my mother would have loved. He pointed out that we're each the driver of our own life's bus. As he talked about how we fuel our ride with positive energy, how we move our bus in the right direction with desire, vision and focus, I saw even more clearly how my mom's example had continued to nourish me. I had faced life without her for years, yet her legacy had been with me. I had not been not alone.

After Jon and I talked for a while, he had the courage to tell me how I could carry on my mother's legacy and lead a more purposeful life through the power of God. He said, "Ben, bring God into your life. Bring Jesus into your life. Lead a purposeful life with the recognition that God had plans for you before the foundation of the Earth." Those plans included an inspirational mother, they also included perseverance, hard work and using my resources to encourage others.

Jon's words got me thinking of other blessings God intentionally put into my life. Even though I was sad that my mother died so young, I realized that God was caring for me when He put me into a family with four wonderful grandparents. Marcel and Bessie, the first generation in their Russian and German families to come to this country, owned a grocery store in St. Louis, Missouri. That store was run on the backs of their own toil, sweat and tears. But they were always available for me, and their example of perseverance had a lasting impact.

Similarly, my grandparents Herman and Shirley modeled many good things, among them a strong marriage. They were married 59 years in 2007 and died 7 days apart, Herman proclaiming that he couldn't live without Shirley. They set a great example of loving well and living each day to its fullest.

Another example they set was honesty. My grandfather Herman strongly believed that a portion of the money each person earns belongs to his family. Yet he failed to create a financial plan to set aside money for the future. When he told me of this failure in an emotional admission, I reassured him that I had never expected an inheritance. But he was emphatic that he'd missed an important opportunity. He advised me to save 10 percent of all I earned for my family. He was firm in saying, "Don't argue with me on this, set that savings aside, because it's your family's money, not your own!"

When I think back, I see many provisions and much wise counsel in my life. Even though I lost my mother at a young age, and spent many years grieving her loss, I now recognize God's hand of provision in so many places in my life.

I am thankful to Jon Gordon for introducing me to a relationship with God and to the truth that God watches over us in ways we might never imagine. I've become a firm believer in the words of 18th-century American psychologist and philosopher William James: "We and God have business with each other and in that business our highest destiny is filled."[2] Since my conversation with Jon, I have read the Holy Bible myself and have discovered Jesus' promise that he would always be with us (Mathew 28:20).

No matter what our circumstances in life, the truth is: We are never alone.

Questions to Ponder:

In spite of your hardships, what good has God provided in your life?

What people have provided the greatest influence?

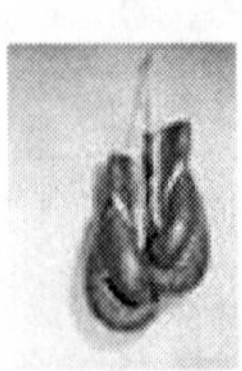

ROUND TWELVE
A Mother's Legacy Lives on

"Though my mother did not include the following scripture from 2 Timothy 4:7 in her journal, I believe these words could be taken to represent the legacy she left me: 'I have fought the good fight, I have finished the race, I have kept the faith.'"

B.A. Newman

When I think of a valuable legacy, I don't think of money or of a stellar reputation. I think of the rich heritage one person can pass to another through examples of love, wise counsel and godly actions.

Though I only enjoyed my mother's parenting for eight short years, she had an impact on me that I'm coming to appreciate more and more as time goes on. I sense that through her example of courage, perseverance and loving kindness, my mother was engraving on my heart something of eternal value. She passed to me a rich inheritance that will stand the test of time. In putting her principles to paper, I proudly share that legacy with you.

It's been amazing to have people approach me with tears

in their eyes, to express the gratitude for kindnesses my mother extended to them over 20 years ago. My wife and I want to live that kind of life and pass those time-tested principles on to our children.

On these final pages, I offer a summary of the principles upon which I am learning to base my life, the principles that usually lead to success but more importantly, principles that model faithfulness.

- Do what you can, with what you have, where you are.
- Realize that what happens to you is not as important as how you respond to it.
- Don't give into denial, self pity or bitterness.
- Understand that obstacles offer opportunities to grow.
- Set long-term goals to keep from being overwhelmed by short-term pressures.
- Stay focused on your "why."
- Remember that good habits make a big difference.
- Know that good habits ***and*** a good attitude make an even bigger difference.
- Surround yourself with great people and learn from them.
- Set excellent standards.
- Analyze challenges and break them into small, do-able pieces.
- Persevere in doing the right thing, despite the threat of rejection or failure.
- Remember that good habits and wise expectations lead to great performance (HELP).
- Embrace adversity head on.
- Charge at your fears like a rhinoceros.
- Read good books, knowing that you become what you feed your mind.
- Don't make excuses; accept responsibility.

- Live the life of a champion by standing up for what is good, right and true.
- Have courageous conversations with important people in your life.
- Examine your worries for self-discovery, revelation and refocus.
- Turn to God for wisdom, comfort and direction.
- Know that He has a purpose for your life.
- Leave the world a better place than you found it.

Most readers are probably already well aware of these principles. However, I know how other people's stories can bring me fresh inspiration. So I offer these precepts from my mother's life so that they may bring enrichment and encouragement wherever needed.

My wish for each reader — and I know it would be my mother's as well — is that you challenge yourself to follow wise disciplines and have a clear vision. By setting high standards and maintaining excellent habits, you will achieve personal and professional freedom and will very likely leave the world a better place than you found it. As you do so, you will be daily rising to the challenge of fighting the good fight.

EPILOGUE BY MARY BESHEAR

"As a mother, I thank God for the treasure of getting to see my own children grow to adulthood. When I look at the fine young man Ben Newman has become, I grieve for the joy Janet Newman has missed, but I also celebrate the legacy she left behind."

Mary Beshear

Our son, Ben, met Ben Newman at a week-long, national, career-training school. The two Bens were roommates who developed great respect for one another. Though their hometowns are 300 miles apart, they have kept in touch, and they continue to encourage and challenge one another, both personally and professionally.

I'd often heard our Ben speak of his friend, but I did not meet Ben Newman until the summer of 2008, when my husband, Ron, and I were attending an annual company meeting with our son. At that meeting, Ben [Beshear] mentioned that his friend was looking for help writing a book. We arranged a quick meeting at the conference, and Ben [Newman] gave me a copy of the outline and chapter proposals for his manuscript.

I was impressed with the way he had organized his work

and with the fact that he already had a website set up to market the yet-unwritten book. However, what really touched me was the fact that he was producing this book to honor his mother. Furthermore, he had a copy of his mother's medical journal, compiled in the last two years of her life. His desire was to take excerpts from her notes and discuss the life principles he found there.

His excitement about honoring his mother was compelling! I think it was Aristotle who said, "Praise invariably implies reference to a higher standard" and encourages excellence all around.[1] One of Aristotle's points was that honor begets honor. And it's true. I was deeply inspired by Ben's tribute to his mom and was moved to help him with it. I was also fascinated and touched that in honoring her, he seemed to want to study her values and thereby come to know her better. When he shared her journal with me, I felt I was holding a treasure.

The pages were mostly filled with medical notes. However, they were her own hand-written notations, compiled at a time of great concern ... a time when she was wondering how long she might be able to continue raising her sons. I could sense her love for them in every one of the copious notes she kept about how to live with and/or conquer amyloidosis.

In August of 2008, Ben Newman and I spent a day together, working through his outline and discussing memories of his mother. As we talked together, memories of my own parents came back to me. Both of them had, before their teen years, experienced the heartbreaking death of their mothers. From my Mom and Dad, I learned that people who experience the early death of a parent will often have far fewer memories than they wish; in fact, sometimes it will be hard to determine which "memories" they do have are fact, and which are fiction. I could see in Ben a desire (similar to that of my parents) to know his mother as a woman. I could also see a desire to know and connect with her values. He was in the process of questioning living relatives about any memories they had concerning his mom. It meant a lot to him when he discovered life principles of hers that underscored his own beliefs and standards.

As I listened to Ben, I saw with compassion and humility that God had placed me in a unique position to be able to help him write this book. I could see his mom with a mother's heart. I was the age his mom would have been, had she lived. I also had a son the same age as hers. I could remember looking at my children when they were Ben's age, wanting to hug them to myself and protect them from every harsh thing that might come their way. I understand a mother's desperation at not being able to completely shield her children.

I also know the joy a mom can feel from a simple story time with her children, or from establishing something that will bless them in the future. In her last months, Janet Newman must have felt so comforted that, long before she'd gotten sick, she had bought a life insurance policy that would enable her sons to go to college.

Another connection I have with Ben Newman is that my son and husband share his profession, so I have great respect for his career. I see the remarkable value he provides clients, and I understand the importance of his basing daily decisions on wise principles. I also know the energy and dedication that go into the company and industry recognition he earns.

As I worked on the book, many days it was with a heavy heart for what Janet missed ...the treasure of getting to nurture her boys and watch them grow into the men God intended them to be. She would be so proud of Ben's career, and she would adore his wife Ami and her own precious grandson, J Isaac.

I marvel at the fine person Ben Newman has become. It's been said that "circumstances are the rulers of the weak, but are the instruments of the wise."[2] That certainly seems true in Ben's case. Here is a young man who could have been bitter over his mother's death and over having to grow up without the unique guidance and comfort that a mother can provide. Instead, he is using energy and resources to honor his mother's memory.

Not only is he taking time to try to extrapolate her values from her medical journal to write this book, but he is also raising money for amyloidosis research. To date, he has raised over $50,000 for ongoing research at Boston Medical Center. Additionally, he has traveled to Boston to give inspirational talks to the medical staff on the difference they make in comforting patients and families.

Though this was not in Janet's notes, one thing I thought as I read her journal was that Andrew and Ben were not only hers , they also belonged to the God of the universe, who has good and wonderful plans for the boys, as He does for each one of us. The Lord of heaven and earth always proves Himself to be what He promised — a shield, a refuge, a comforter and a restorer of the soul. God brings joy in the midst of pain quite beautifully, too.

One of the delightfully serendipitous moments for Ben in recent months was the discovery that Dr. Martha Skinner, now director of amyloidosis research at Boston Medical Center, happened to be the beloved Dr. Skinner mentioned in his mom's journal 20 years ago. I was thrilled to be one of the first people Ben called to share the excitement of that connection. After Ben and Dr. Skinner made that discovery, Dr Skinner was able to share with Ben the files she had kept on his mother. It was a momentous connection with his past that supplied one more association with the mother he lost so long ago.

It has been my pleasure to help Ben write this book. I believe Janet Newman was a delightful woman and mother; I also sense she is someone I would have loved having as a friend. So, I was deeply touched when Ben told me that the words we have written together have helped make his mother more knowable to him, to his wife, Ami, and (someday) to their son, J. Isaac.

As is usually the case with a labor of love, multiple blessings have flowed my way, as well. Janet Newman's story has prompted me to see the priceless moments I sometimes miss around me. As a wife and mother, for example, I think about all the times I have been impatient, tired, or distracted with less important things. Looking at Janet's last years, when each moment was precious, I have gained a new appreciation for the value of giving my worries to God each day and trying to live more in the present with family and loved ones.

Question to Ponder:

Given the brevity of our days on earth, what can we each do on a regular basis to be more present for the important people in our lives?

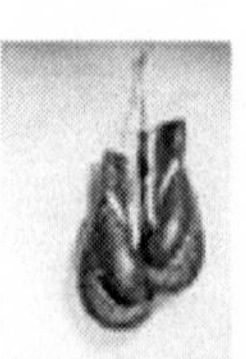

Questions to Ponder:

1. *Are there worthwhile endeavors needing to be done around you that you could easily accomplish with your current resources and within your existing circumstances?*

2. *What circumstances and obstacles have molded your life?*

3. *What steps have you taken to get beyond the obstacles?*

4. *What quiet characteristics might be lying within you, waiting for an affirmation or verbal description that can bring them to life?*

5. *Can you put these traits into words, words that might somehow help you better act on them?*

6. *What is your "why" your purpose beyond yourself?*

7. *What are you doing to ensure that you fulfill this purpose?*

8. *How are you stretching yourself in order to improve?*

9. *What defining moments in your life have revealed your inner desires in sharper focus?*

10. *What principles have provided wise "guardrails" as you embarked on a new endeavor?*

11. *What obstacles seem to be holding you back right now?*

12. *What areas of your life might be in need of stretching and growth?*

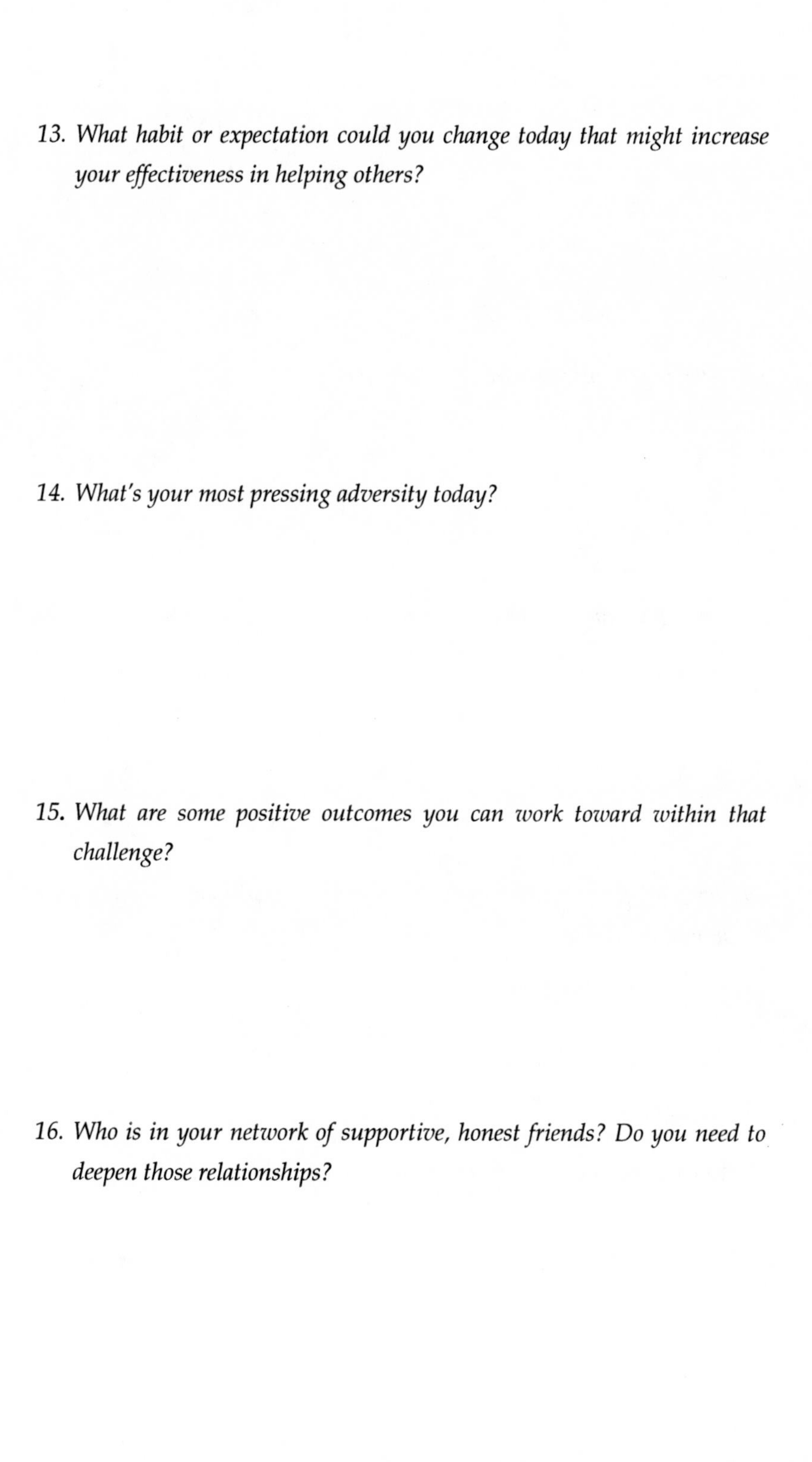

13. *What habit or expectation could you change today that might increase your effectiveness in helping others?*

14. *What's your most pressing adversity today?*

15. *What are some positive outcomes you can work toward within that challenge?*

16. *Who is in your network of supportive, honest friends? Do you need to deepen those relationships?*

17. *How will the decisions you make today impact your future?*

18. *What are the principles of your daily fight?*

19. *Are you accepting responsibility for your actions in your life?*

20. *Based on your talents, standards and values, what's worth setting your mind's eye on?*

21. *What steps do you want to take to bring your vision to life?*

22. *What keeps you up at night and what are you doing about it?*

23. *In spite of your hardships, what good has God provided in your life?*

24. *What people have provided the greatest influence?*

25. *Given the brevity of our days on earth, what might you do on a regular basis to be more present to the important people in your life?*

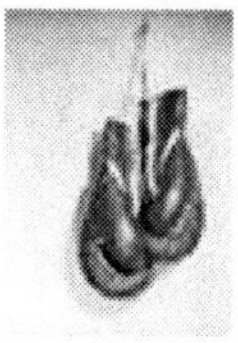

Notes

Round One: Be a Prizefighter

1. Wynn Davis, comp. The Best of Success: *A Treasury of Success Ideas (Lombard,* Illinois; 1992), p. 293.
2. Ibid., p. 294.

Round Two: A Mother's Journal

1. Sidney Greenberg, ed. A Treasury of the Art of Living (Hollywood, California; 1963), p. 178.

Round Three: Why? Discovering Your Purpose

1. Jim Tressel, The Winner's Manual: *for the Game of Life* (Carol Stream, Illinois; 2008), p. 39.
2. Scott Smiley, "Soldier of the Year," Guideposts Magazine (August, 2008), pp. 50-55.
3. Rick Warren, The Purpose Driven Life: *What on Earth Am I here for? (*Grand Rapids, Michigan; 2002), p. 319.

Round Four: Defining Moments

1. Jim Rohn, *Excerpts from* The Treasury of Quotes (Irving, Texas; 1993), p. 23.
2. Ibid.

Round Five: Courage in Pursuit of Capacity

1. John C. Maxwell, The 360-Degree Leader (Nashville, 2005), p. 153.
2. Mike Kennedy and Mark Stewart, "Jockbio: Michael Phelps Biography" (Jockbio.com,2008).
3. Peggy Anderson, comp. Great Quotes from Great Leaders (Lombard, Illinois; 1990), p. 19.
4. Davis, The Best of Success, p. 256

Round Six: Help

1. Greenberg, A Treasury of the Art of Living, p. 194.
2. Ibid., p. 200.
3. Maxwell, The 360-Degree Leader, p. 162.

Round Seven: Embrace the Adversity

1. Davis, The Best of Success, p. 67.
2. Scott Alexander, Rhinoceros Success (Laguna Hills, California; 1980), p. 18.
3. Ibid., p. 31.
4. Tressel, The Winner's Manual, p. 153.

Round Eight: The Daily Fight

1. Vince Lombardi, What it Takes to be Number 1: *Vince Lombardi On leadership* (New York, 2001), p. 51.
2. Davis, The Best of Success, p. 44.
3. Anderson, Great Quotes from Great Leaders, p. 3.
4. Ibid., p. 89.

Round Nine: Mind's Eye

1. Davis, The Best of Success, p. 325.

Round Ten: What Keeps You Up at Night?

1. Dr. Martha Skinner's letter to Herman Fishman, Dec 17, 1986.
2. Greenberg, A Treasury of the Art of Living, p. 126.
3. Tressel, The Winner's Manual, p. 232.

Round Eleven: You are Never Alone

1. Warren, The Purpose Driven Life, p. 233.
2. Greenberg, A Treasury of the Art of Living, p. 333.

Epilogue

1. Greenberg, A Treasury of the Art of Living, p. 96.
2. Davis, The Best of Success, p. 265.

ABOUT THE AUTHORS

Benjamin Newman

Benjamin Newman is a life insurance salesman in St. Louis, Missouri. In addition, Ben is the founder and a motivational speaker with The Continued Fight, LLC (**www.continuedfight.com**), a company that works with organizations in overcoming challenges to seek positive outcomes in their futures.

In his career in the insurance industry, Ben has qualified for the Million Dollar Roundtable every year he has been in the business. In March of 2008 and in March of 2009, Ben was recognized as one of the **Wealth Managers of the Year in "St. Louis Magazine." In addition, in 2008 and 2009, Ben qualified for an elite group within his company and is ranked in its top 2 percent of all representatives (10,000 total) in the U.S.**

As an activist in the search for the cure for amyloidosis, Ben has raised over $50,000 since 2005 and philanthropically donates a portion of the proceeds from his speaking engagements to the Boston Medical Center for Research and the Children's Miracle Network of St. Louis. He also currently sits on the Board of Directors of Youth Lifeline of America, a non-profit organization based in St. Louis.

Ben's most important goals in life are continued happiness, love, spirituality and continued self improvement as he and his wife, Ami, grow their family, beginning with their son, J. Isaac, who was born on March 4, 2008, all the while embodying his belief that the essence of leadership is leading by example.

Mary Beshear

A former co-host of the daily radio program, *A Gift of Encouragement,* Mary Beshear says that the thing she enjoys most as a wife, mother, writer and speaker is finding ways to encourage family, friends and co-workers.

Before completing a Ph.D. at Marquette University, Mary taught high-school English and enjoyed the opportunity to encourage teens in the skills of critical thinking, creative writing and confident public speaking. After she and her husband Ron were blessed with children, she applied her nurturing gifts at home with son Ben and daughter Robin.

Over the years, Mary has served on various trustee boards, including: Cincinnati Hills Christian Academy, Vineyard Community Church and the Advisory Board for the Cincinnati Healing Center. She also had the pleasure of serving as Woman's Co-chair for the 2002 Billy Graham Mission event in Cincinnati. In each of these offices, Mary says her goal has been to bring prayer support, encouragement and compassionate wisdom to the board and committee tables.

In addition to board service, Mary currently leads Bible studies for women in the Cincinnati community. She has written two other books, ***The One HE Loves,*** an inspirational Bible study for women, and ***Fall in Love with Your Future,*** a short motivational book that she coauthored with her husband, Ron. For more information on Mary, visit: **www.ServingYourPurpose.com**.